# Walking to Wachusett

# Walking to Wachusett

A Re-enactment of Henry David Thoreau's

## *A Walk to Wachusett*

Robert M. Young

Young, Robert M., 1945–

Walking to Wachusett: a re-enactment of Henry David Thoreau's "A Walk to Wachusett"

Summary: Walk with the author along Thoreau's route taken in 1842 from Concord, Massachusetts to the summit of Mount Wachusett in Princeton, Massachusetts. Experience today's landscape, compare and contrast it with that of Thoreau's day. Includes bibliographical references and index.

The copy text for "A Walk to Wachusett" is from the Princeton University Press 2007 Edition of *Excursions.*

ISBN 978-0-615-26408-0

1. Thoreau, Henry David, 1817-1862 —Naturalist – History – In literature – Wachusett – Transcendentalism – New England. 2. New England —Transportation – Road System. 3. Massachusetts — Princeton – Mount Wachusett. I. Title.



First Edition

Published by Robert M. Young
8 Lynnhaven Road
Leominster, Massachusetts 01453

Contact: ryoung@alumni.unc.edu

Printer: LuLu.com

Book Photography: Howard Kong

Front Cover: Along Route 117, the Great Road, in Stow.
Back Cover: Orchard along Route 117 in Stow.
Title Page: Mountain House Trail, Mount Wachusett, Princeton.

## Dedication

This work is dedicated to two very special persons, both of whom have had considerable impact upon my avocation as a writer.

To my high school English teacher, Mr. Delevan E. Whaley Jr. Every child should have such a learning experience, and … I never even knew it was happening. You got me started long ago; may you rest in peace.

To my dear wife, Kathleen. I am so fortunate to be wed to such a concerned and caring woman. You experienced this project from the beginning to the end—listening, reading, editing, discussing, and suggesting. Your patience and encouragement kept me going. We had a good trip together. I couldn't have done it without you.

# Contents

## Acknowledgments

Throughout this project, I have encountered many fine and wonderful folks, eager to lend a hand or an encouraging word. As I would find along the journey, good people are encountered everywhere. With fear of leaving a helpful hand un-named, I salute and thank the following: Ms. Mary Lynch Cadwallader of the Princeton Historical Society, Mr. Jeffrey Cramer of The Thoreau Institute at Walden Woods, Mr. David Gibbs of the Sterling Historical Society, Professor William Howarth of Princeton University, Ms. Constance Manoli-Skocay of the Special Collections Department of The Concord Free Public Library, Professor Joseph Moldenhauer of the University of Texas at Austin, Professor Henrik Otterberg of the University of Gothenburg, Sweden, Ms. Susan Paju (and staff) at the Acton Memorial Library, Professor Robert Sattelmeyer of Georgia State University, and Dr. Elizabeth Hall Witherell of University of California at Santa Barbara.

And for one very special person whose footprints are indelibly inscribed onto this project: my neighbor, Mr. Howard Kong, a good friend and an exceptional photographer, without whom the pictorial content of the project would never have come to pass. He followed me for miles and miles, throughout the whole trip, unobtrusively but happily clicking away. The result speaks for itself.

# Introduction

Henry David Thoreau's essay "A Walk to Wachusett" had never been re-enacted when I first read it in 2002! A curious type, I read the essay and was left with an obvious question to ponder: over what route did he travel as he made his journey from Concord to Wachusett? By 2005 I had learned that some before me had pieced together projected routes; some had followed that activity by driving their chosen route; one hearty individual attempted the walk on foot (his feet gave out in Stow); and another made a symbolic walk over an extended timeframe, starting in West Concord. But nowhere was I able to find a satisfying response: documentation of a historically correct route and a record of an actual transit of that route on foot.

*Walking to Wachusett* is my response. I walked as closely as I might to his very footsteps; I recorded my thoughts as I walked, and then I wrote my testimony. I wrote it in an effort to fill this apparent void in the archives and the body of knowledge concerning one of America's greatest naturalists: Henry David Thoreau. And if, perchance, the records exist and we simply did not cross paths, I can only say that it has been a wonderful sojourn back to the past.

The year 1842 was a turning point in Thoreau's life. Only five years removed from Harvard College, Thoreau spent the ensuing years working to craft his niche in life. From teacher, to pencil-maker, to poet, to orator, to tutor, to traveler, to handyman, he had not yet discovered how to garner a living and, at the same time, to fulfill his passion for writing.

Early in the year, as his career as a poet was gaining momentum, two events seemed to turn his fortune. On January 12, older brother John passed away, suddenly afflicted with lockjaw caused by a razor cut, and just 15 days later, Waldo, the young son of mentor R.W. Emerson, passed away due to complications of scarlet fever. Severe

erson, passed away due to complications of scarlet fever. Severe losses for Thoreau—he had loved each dearly. Thoreau was in shock; the hands of grief wrapped securely about him. It was a short but difficult struggle.

By March, his recovery was underway. The corner had been turned and fortune smiled on him. With a sudden burst of creative energy his most popular writing style germinated. What probably began as a muse in memory of John, turned out to be the travelogue. Although he and John had traveled to Mt. Washington in 1839, a trip that later gave birth to *A Week On The Concord and Merrimack Rivers*, it was his walk to Mt. Wachusett that laid the foundation for the excursion essays.

But, make no mistake, this was more than just a four day summertime walk with student Richard Fuller to a mountain 35 miles distant; it was a walk back in history to the Indian Wars, to the ages of gold, silver and bronze, to the Trojan War; it was a walk about New England and the north-east and also to far places of the globe—to South America, to France, to Italy, to England, to Rome, to Egypt, to the Canary Islands of coastal Africa, to the mystical world of Arabia, and to the stars and planets of the celestial world beyond. It was a journey taken with a variety of companions—Wordsworth, Virgil, Humboldt, Homer, Emerson, "Robin Hood", farmers, pedestrians and local residents. Above all, it was an expedition, the first of many in search of what might lie to the undiscovered west and his term for the destination: the wild.

# Walkers, Writers, and Riders

Research turned no leaf of a completed effort to re-enact the 1842 journey of Thoreau and Harvard College student Richard Fuller as described in Thoreau's essay "A Walk to Wachusett". Nor did I discover any detailed description of their precise route. What I did find however, are a number of *suggested* routes and automobile drives which chart courses that they *may have taken.* Since Thoreau left but few clues of the route they traveled, these trips are best taken in spirit rather than in preciseness and in exactness.

You may discover that, unbeknown to you, a Sunday drive in the country may have taken you along parts of his route. A fruit stand with which you are familiar or even your home might rest along the route. Close your eyes; think back to dirt roads and the days of "horse and buggy;" imagine the possibilities.

In chronological order of their outings to Wachusett, I found the following persons to have made the trip to Wachusett. With the exception of the first, who was merely traveling to the interior of the Commonwealth, these individuals were seeking a more complete understanding of this early excursion of Thoreau.

### The Reverend Thomas Prince

Perhaps one of the earliest journeys from the eastern environs of Cambridge and Boston to Worcester County and the mountain area of Wachusett is reported in Francis Everett Blake's *History of Princeton.* The Reverend Thomas Prince, after whom Princeton takes its name, often traveled between Boston and the interior lands of Worcester County in the early 1700s. Blake writes of Prince:

> One can trace his probable route as he left his home in Boston for one of his trips to the interior. He would pass perhaps through Cambridge and

> Waltham to Sudbury where he could greet his brother minister and perhaps be entertained over night. In the morning he would follow the old traveled road to Lancaster, at that period a frequently used country road. At Lancaster he would find another brother in the ministry, a college friend whose entertainment he might prefer to the inn. From Lancaster he would pass through Chocksett, now Sterling, then into the path used by occasional travelers in that direction. By this time he would find dwellings few and far between, especially when he reached the area now included in our town [Princeton]. From this point doubtless the road was very rough and as there was no settlement or even occasional houses he had to depend upon his own resources for rest and refreshment.[1]

So, while we may consider Thoreau's trip in 1842 to be somewhat of a groundbreaking venture, we find that this general route was well established long before Thoreau's time. Tracing the route taken by Prince, it would be along the Lancaster Road to Bolton (now Route 117) and then a secondary country road to Lancaster and Sterling. Blake reports the obvious western look in and about Princeton.

**William Howarth**

Several guidebooks have been written addressing the mountain travels of Thoreau. First published as *Thoreau in the Mountains*,[2] William Howarth's revised book, *Walking with Thoreau*,[3] provides an excellent discussion of Thoreau's travels away from his comfort zone of

---

[1] Francis Everett Blake, *History of Princeton Massachusetts* vol. I, (Boston: Blake, 1915) 114–115.

[2] Henry David Thoreau, *Thoreau in the Mountains: A Literary Guide to the Mountains of New England,* commentary by William Howarth. (New York: Farrar Straus Giroux, 1982).

[3] Henry David Thoreau, *Walking with Thoreau,* commentary by William Howarth (Boston: Beacon Press, 2001).

Concord. Included is the celebrated journey to Wachusett. Howarth drove his route to the mountain with friends[4] from Concord and then hiked to the summit on the Old Indian Trail, the northern approach. Accordingly, his route is fashioned along modern highways, some of which were quite active and vibrant in 1842. While it is very close to my chosen route, there are differences, especially in the section of Concord-Acton-Stow and the final climb to the summit.

The beginning of Howarth's route is more westerly as it follows Route 2 to Route 111 and West Acton before reaching Route 117. My chosen path follows the old Lancaster Road, now Route 117, from Concord all the way to Stow and Bolton. On the approach to the summit, the choice automobile ride is to the northern side of the mountain while I believe Thoreau approached from the east and his defined "base of the mountain."

**James Kruger**

Situated on a hillside a short distance from Walden Pond, I found the Thoreau Institute at the end of a narrow winding side road. There, in a striking wood paneled public study, I read James Kruger's essay, "Walk to Wachusetts[sic]," the story of his adventure walk taken in the summer of 1985.[5] On vacation and with little time available for preparation, research was conducted in a just a few days with assistance from the staff at The Concord Free Public Library. Finally, having established his route, he set out early one morning as had Thoreau and Fuller. Kruger obviously had the right idea; he went afoot.

---

[4] William Howarth, email received 6/24/2004.

[5] Articles of interest from The Thoreau Institute at Walden Woods, including Kruger's essay, were in Box 174, the Walter Harding Collection as retrieved by Curator Jeffrey Cramer when I visited in September 2004. The folder is now listed in the Walter Harding Collection as Series II.5.c.3.a–d.

Unfortunately, upon reaching Stow, the halfway point of the trip, blisters overcame his already tired feet, and his wife was forced to enact a rescue. Following recuperation of a few days, he resumed his journey by automobile. But even in the failed attempt, one learns from Kruger a valuable lesson about Thoreau, and perhaps, in general, of all citizens in that time period. They were in excellent physical shape; forced perhaps by the earthy lifestyle that they lived.

For the valiant attempt, it is unfortunate that his chosen route is not well documented. After many hours of research, his essay reveals very little of the route that he determined to have been taken by Thoreau and Fuller. Nevertheless, he did leave one valuable hint by mentioning "Old Stow Road" and the Fitchburg Railroad tracks. That is indeed an important location along the route especially since a major portion of that road was abandoned with the construction of the railway in 1844. He also confirms that he walked the Great Road, Prince's Lancaster Road (Rt. 117), to reach Bolton, but beyond that, little is revealed of his planned route. It was a good, well-intended effort; it simply gave way to the peril of walking long distances when not physically prepared.

**Lynnwood Erskine**

Ms. Mary Lynch Cadwallader, curator of the Princeton Historical Society found it to be quite amazing that within the course of a couple of weeks in the spring of 2006, she met two individuals who could affirm that they had walked Thoreau's route from Concord to Wachusett. One was myself; the other was Mr. Lynnwood Erskine.

I called Mr. Erskine on the telephone. An elderly gentleman who lives in the local area, he recalled that his college roommate, now deceased, was the inspiration behind their walk, which was taken in about 1996. Mr. Erskine recalls few details of the journey inasmuch as the college roommate was the pathfinder. But what he does recall is significant: they started the trip from West Concord where his friend lived, they returned home each night, they took three days to arrive at the mountain, and they followed the reservation's commercial road to reach the summit. None of these proposals is reflected in "A Walk to Wachusett."

Erskine was impressed by the magnitude of Thoreau's effort; he repeatedly asked whether I had completed my walk in "Thoreau Time," alluding to one's walking speed on the road.

In the course of talking with Mr. Erskine, he revealed a true Thoreauvian spirit within his soul. He told of extended overland walks taken in his younger days and recommended that I think about walking the path taken by Mary Rowlandson and her captors, the Nipmunk and Narragansett Indians during King Phillip's War. She was taken from her home in Lancaster and released near the shores of Wachusett Pond in 1776.

I must say that Erskine's walk was a solid effort, but it was not the full re-enactment for which I was searching.

**Michael Tougias**

By his own admission, Tougias' essay, "Thoreau's Wachusett,"[6] is a quest in search of the spirit of Thoreau. While he scans "topographical maps spread before me, trying to guess Thoreau's path," the plotted path, once again, is made for driving. Pensive musings of a sojourner who has found the beauty of Wachusett it is, and while Tougias definitely succeeds in his purpose, the definitive route in

---

[6] Michael J. Tougias, *New England Wild Places* (North Attleborough, Massachusetts: Covered Bridge Press, 1997) 72.

question cannot to be found in this selection.

**J. Parker Huber**

As part of a series called *The Spirit of Thoreau*, sponsored by the *Thoreau Society*, J. Parker Huber edits a collection of Thoreau writings about his journeys to the mountains of the northeast titled *Elevating Ourselves: Thoreau on Mountains.*[7] Huber relates to the spirit of Thoreau in his travels—what he sought, what he learned, and what he passes on to us in the 21st century. While this is an excellent choice for reading about Thoreau and his out-of-doors activities, there is no mention of the specific route traveled to Wachusett beyond the essay itself and Thoreau's words.

**The Others**

There are probably more accounts; I just never found them. While researching the subject at the Thoreau Institute, I came across the following hand-written note on the back of a map drawn by H.F. Walling; it had no date and no originator.

> Rt. 111 to West Acton, Willow Street to West Acton Road to Stow; 117 Stow to Bolton to South Lancaster to Ebenville to Redstone Hill to Sterling Center, West Sterling, E. Princeton. Back to Ster Center to Ebenville to South Lancaster, to Still River to Harvard Center to Boxboro to West Acton.[8]

It's not my route, but starting in Concord, it's also not a bad itinerary to reach Wachusett. Someone was definitely thinking about the

[7] J. Parker Huber, ed., *Elevating Ourselves: Thoreau on Mountains* (Boston: Houghton Mifflin, 1999).

[8] Unknown author; pencil note found on the back of a map by HF Walling, 98 Trowbridge St., Cambridge, Mass., no date. The map was located in the "A Walk to Wachusett" file folder at the Institute–Box 174.

route and what might have been. I was unfamiliar with the name Ebenville, and it took a while to find, but I did. No longer a well-recognized village, it is situated right on my selected route, in Lancaster.[9]

So, perhaps somewhere there is a published manuscript; perhaps a scholar has written a dissertation; or there may exist documentation written by an amateur historian like myself that lies in a hot, dusty attic of a home in the vicinity. For now, I have nothing but my own story. I hope you enjoy.

[9] 21 miles from Concord. Coordinates: 42°26'16" N, 71°42' 04" W.

# My Search Begins

The large velvet covered chain snapped shut behind me, and down the metal staircase I descended into the bowels of the Leominster Public Library. A hollow echo sounded loudly with each step. Near the bottom, I squinted into the alcove dimly lit with two frosted low wattage bulbs. A musty smell filled my nostrils, not offensive, just stuffy and stale. There was the reference collection. Several bookshelves, one desk upon which one might spread work papers, and two chairs—one surely to serve as a coat rack—filled the dank claustrophobic space. Glamorous, it was not, but if I could find what I was looking for, none of that would matter.

Quite by accident and before I removed my jacket, I spied an atlas on the bottom shelf right in front of me, the *Atlas of Worcester County* published originally by the F. W. Beers Co. in 1870. It was almost 30 years after Thoreau's walk, but it was a place to begin my search for maps, artifacts, and documents that might reveal the route taken by Thoreau and Fuller in 1842.

The project was, one might say, officially underway. But, exactly what was the project and from what did it originate?

Several years back, while doing research for a trip to climb Mount Katahdin, in Maine, I came across several references to American philosopher and naturalist Henry David Thoreau that described the time he spent traveling about the wilderness areas of Maine many years ago. I was impressed; he is definitely remembered for his travels in that area. With my interest piqued, I did some extended reading and came across an essay of his that, to put it mildly, struck a cord: "A Walk to Wachusett."

I began to realize that my friend Thoreau and I shared a common bond—a love of the outdoors and what it freely offers us daily. A friendship was rekindled.

He begins:

> The needles of the pine,
> All to the west incline.
>
> CONCORD, JULY 19, 1842.
>
> SUMMER and winter our eyes had rested on the dim outline of the mountains in our horizon, to which distance and indistinctness lent a grandeur not their own, so that they served equally to interpret all the allusions of poets and travellers; whether with Homer, on a spring morning, we sat down on the many-peaked Olympus, or, with Virgil, and his compeers, roamed the Etrurian and Thessalian hills, or with Humboldt measured the more modern Andes and Teneriffe. Thus we spoke our mind to them, standing on the Concord cliffs.–[10]

Fascinating! Initially, I simply wanted to know his exact route from Concord to Wachusett; later I sensed that there was more to it than just knowledge of a passageway from one point to another. I wanted to see, to smell, and to feel what he saw, what he smelled and what he felt on the road to Wachusett 167 years ago.

I pondered the essay as a complete body of work; I read and re-read each paragraph, carefully examining the words of every sentence. Dictionaries, maps, and research texts were perused in order to extract the precise intention of everything he wrote about the trip. My knowledge of and familiarity with the immediate countryside helped, and a multitude of treks to the summit provided an anchor for understanding the destination. But even with that as background, some-

---

10 Henry David Thoreau, *Excursions*, ed. Joseph J. Moldenhauer (Princeton: Princeton UP, 2007) 29.2–15.

thing was absent; my understanding was partial and incomplete. What about *this*, and what about *that*? What did he mean by using *this word* or *that word*? Suppose he took *this route*; suppose he took *that route*? Each question must have an answer that could be proven beyond a shadow of doubt. If I knew those answers, how then, might I interpret his words? What would it tell me? Are there any lessons here or is it just a 19th century travelogue? Had necessary details been omitted? Was Thoreau careless in his writing? Should I not believe what he wrote? Did it really happen as he wrote it? Were any incidents fabricated? Exactly what was it like along the road? The simple quest was growing legs … fast.

And there was more. Soon, I began to wonder if there was anything left of the 19th century. Was the landscape retrievable? Could I find a slice of what, at that time in the history of our country, was the norm—the agrarian society and the infrastructure that supported it? Could his walk tell me anything about living in the twenty-first century?

Basic assumptions became clear as my study continued, or perhaps they were hypotheses picked along the roadside much like the berries picked by Thoreau and Fuller. I had to start somewhere.

**Assumption 1.** Passage was made either "on" or in "close proximity" to established common roads of the day.

While it is well documented that Thoreau enjoyed walking in fields, meadows, woods and swamps of surrounding towns, there are a sufficient number of references to "roads" in the essay for me to believe that, on this trip, he followed the course of established roads of the day. He writes early on of the passage through Acton and Stow: "we moved happily along the dank roads." Leaving West Sterling, he describes the route: "Our road lay along the course of the

Stillwater," and soon thereafter, he commented on "the raspberries, which grew abundantly by the roadside." Finally, leaving the summit, "we plodded along the dusty roads."

That is not to say that they never took an occasional shortcut through meadows or pastures; I believe they probably did. In fact he wrote: "we strolled into the woods and along the course of a rivulet" as they passed through Lancaster, all the while, not far from the Post Road.

Yes, definitely, this trip was taken "on dusty roads."

**Assumption 2.** The route included only those towns or villages specifically noted in the essay.

Written in the format of a travelogue, Thoreau mentions several towns through which they passed: Concord, Acton, Stow, Bolton, Lancaster, Sterling (including West Sterling), and Princeton (location of the summit) to reach Wachusett. On departure from the summit, the sequence as written is: Princeton, Sterling (West Sterling or Stillwater), Lancaster, Still River Village, Harvard, and Concord. From Harvard, Fuller continued north to Groton[11] while Thoreau returned to Concord.

Keeping in mind the towns mentioned by Thoreau in juxtaposition with his written word, one can decipher significant clues about the route. For example: having reached Bolton just before noon and overlooking the valley of Lancaster, he writes, "the lay of the land hereabouts is well worthy the attention of the traveller." And then he describes the geography before him, specifying rivers by name and description, distances in miles, compass directions, and nearby towns.

[11] His parents lived in Groton from 1833 to 1837; his father passed away in 1835. At the time of the journey to Wachusett, an uncle lived in Groton.

From this information, he is easily pictured resting comfortably atop Watoquadoc Hill.

There is, I must confess, one obvious exception to the rule. Leaving Harvard, depending upon their exact resting place for the night of the 21st, Thoreau would have passed through either Boxborough or Littleton in order to return to Concord. Neither town is mentioned in the essay. My theory is that from the center of Harvard, a return would have been made by the shortest route—the Road to Concord, later called the Harvard Turnpike and now Route 111—directly to West Acton and on to Concord.

**Assumption 3.** The route taken between two points was the most direct that headed in a westerly direction.

At various junctions, there might have been more than one way to go from point A to point B. Since there is often little or no detail upon which to base a decision, I generally walked along the shortest primary road that headed in the westerly direction. An overview of a map also helped gauge the *flow* of the route.

For example, leaving Lancaster, it would have been quite possible to take Redstone Hill Road to Sterling. On the other hand, the route that I favor for this section of the trip is that of the old Post Road; it's direct and it runs nicely from Common Village headed west to Sterling. It was good enough for the postal carriages; it surely was sufficient for Thoreau.

Another section of the route where this assumption plays a role is upon leaving Sterling on the Post Road over Fitch's Hill. At the crest of the hill Thoreau could have taken the left hand fork (toward Princeton) for two miles. Reaching the Stillwater River (Moore's Corners), he would have then turned north along the Post Road to Westminster for the final mile to reach West Sterling. On the other hand, at the crest Fitch's Hill, he could have taken the right hand fork—Beamon Road—and walked directly to West Sterling, a distance of two miles. This latter option is more appealing because it is shorter, by about a mile, and also because Beamon Road runs all the way to the "base of the mountain."

*****

More study; more trips to the library, more books … and yet, it still wasn't coming together.

Thoreau thought it impossible to fully understand another person unless there existed some parallel thread of life along which they had both traveled. He wrote, "for knowledge is to be acquired only by a corresponding experience. How can we *know* what we are *told* merely? Each man can interpret another's experience only by his own."[12] According to this precept, my interpretation of his experience was limited by my own experience. Separated by years of societal, economic, technological, and political change, I apparently faced a monstrous constraint, and only with a convergence of experiences, might my interpretation inherit some degree of validity.

R. G. Collingwood, the English philosopher, historian and archaeologist wrote: "the mere fact that someone has expressed his thoughts in writing, and that we possess his works, does not enable us to understand his thoughts. In order that we may be able to do so, we must come to the reading of them prepared with an experience sufficiently like his own to make those thoughts organic to it."[13] Very

---

12 Henry David Thoreau, *A Week on the Concord and Merrimack Rivers,* (Princeton: Princeton UP, 1980) 365.4–7.

13 R.G. Collingwood, *The Idea of History,* ed. Jan Van Der Dussen, Revised Edition (Oxford: Oxford University Press, 1994) 300.

much like the words of Thoreau.

Therefore, on the advice of these two scholars, I arrived at the following conclusion: if I wished to understand Thoreau's journey completely, with no questions, and with no room for doubt, the *scissors-and-paste historical method*, while it would provide guidance and assistance in reconstructing the journey, would not suffice; a reenactment of the journey was clearly the only option for obtaining unqualified evidence that supported any conclusions of his endeavor.[14]

The approach was now to gather leaves of history before they returned to the soil. My wife's words were direct and much more to the point, and she didn't have to study scholarly references: "you have to walk it yourself."

* * * * *

But, first remember words written early in the essay:

> At length, like Rasselas, and other inhabitants of happy valleys, we resolved to scale the blue wall which bound the western horizon, though not without misgivings, that thereafter no visible fairy land would exist for us.[15]

For me as I walk, and you too, as you read, there will be no visible fairyland waiting at the end of the journey. That fairyland will be gone forever. The only one remaining will be over the next mountaintop and that is a choice for each of us to make. Thoreau and Fuller chose to go; I choose to go; I hope you will too. Let us be away ....

---

[14] Collingwood, 282.

[15] Thoreau, *Excursions*, 31.18–22.

# August 2005: The Re-Enactment

AFOOT and light-hearted I take to the open road,
Healthy, free, the world before me,
The long brown path before me leading wherever I choose.
Henceforth I ask not good-fortune, I myself am good-fortune,
Henceforth I whimper no more, postpone no more, need nothing,
Done with indoor complaints, libraries, querulous criticisms,
Strong and content I travel the open road.

*From "Song of the Open Road" by Walt Whitman*

## *4:45 A.M. EDT Saturday, August 6, 2005—Concord, MA*

The dark of night cast its shadows as the piercing headlights of an oncoming vehicle bounced through the blackness of the Cambridge Turnpike just beyond Concord center. Quickly, the lights spun 180° and came to a halt just past "The Emerson House." The lights were extinguished, and two figures emerged, one slowly pulling a large pack from within, the other quickly moving down the street and peering through the lens of a camera mounted upon a steadying tripod. The first, now with the pack mounted securely upon his back, crossed the street and paused before the closed front gate of the property. The rapid fire clicking of a high-speed camera shutter penetrated the quiet; the two figures gathered in conference, shook hands and parted.

It was Saturday, August 6, 2005 and the time was 4:45 a.m. EDT. Along with my good friend, photographer Howard Kong, I had just left the *R.W. Emerson House*, an historic landmark affectionately called *Bush*[16] by its owner. My purpose was singular: to re-enact the 1842 journey of Henry David Thoreau and his companion Richard Fuller

[16] W. Barksdale Maynard, *Walden Pond, A History* (New York: Oxford University Press, 2004), 30.

as they sought to "scale the blue wall which bounded the western horizon" approximately 36 miles distant in Princeton, Massachusetts: Mount Wachusett. Starting at the same early morning time[17] as my predecessors, I would retrace their steps, as closely as possible and according to a rough timeline that matched theirs. By nightfall I would reach West Sterling, just below the base of the mountain, and tomorrow, atop the summit, I would scan the horizon and gaze over Concord resting to the east. Might I find relics of the past as Thoreau encountered them? Perhaps I would find nothing; perhaps I would encounter the gods of Wachusett, or ghosts of the west.

Aside from the dual ping of hiking poles scratching the macadam road surface, the first sound of the morning came as a surprise: "Bong ... Bong ... Bong ... Bong ... Bong." A bell tower[18] from somewhere high in the sky eerily sounded the hour as I strode along the Lexington Road toward Concord Center. It was only moments before, in the predawn darkness that I had left the front gate of Bush. Like Thoreau and Fuller, I too, turned left and marched toward the Center. We were together now, separated by 163 years! If all went well with our journey, we would be *brothers of the road* in three days.

At this early hour, I could see no further than the street lights would allow, barely making out the houses, churches and other buildings that lie off the roadside. Just before the rotary that marks the center of town, I passed what I later learned was the source of the pealing bells—First Parish.[19]

---

[17] Today we follow Daylight Savings Time–first adopted in the United States on March 19, 1918. Had it been 1842, the time would have been 3:45 a.m.

[18] First Parish (Unitarian Universalist Church). The bell was manufactured by E. Howard & Co. of Boston (ca. 1900). Information provided by Doug Baker, Sacristan and Curator.

[19] Doug Baker, Email to author dated 8/29/2005.

### *5:10 A.M.—Main Street, Concord*

Pausing momentarily at the rotary, I gazed straight ahead down an isolated Main Street and felt, as on a pedestal, a conductor of the orchestra about to announce the opening act of the show. In fact, that's exactly what I was doing. In spite of my own excitement as conductor of the day's performance, a perfectly quiet town slumbered peacefully behind the dim glow of streetlights. No one stirred save those of us who had obligations: two bakers hard at work on the business end of their establishments, a middle aged man shuffling through empty waste barrels on the north side of the street and me, a sojourner, just passing through.

The first three, I was sure, would remain for the day; I would continue, step by step, through Concord, on to Acton and in succession, as a train conductor might bellow: Stow, Bolton, Lancaster, Sterling, West Sterling, East Princeton and Waaaaaaachusett Mountain. But there would be many steps before that arrival could be announced. For now, I continued down Main Street, formerly known as Lancaster Road.

Passing 100 Main Street, I noticed the first cemetery of the day, South Burying Place, located just before the "new" Concord Academy. For some strange reason, and I really don't know why, I kept watch for the cemeteries. I suppose it might have been due to the fact that, with dated headstones, I might learn whether a particular plot of land was in use when Thoreau and Fuller passed by. In fact, neither Thoreau nor Fuller made any mention in their writing of cemeteries passed during the trip. Perhaps it was just a connection in some morbid fashion, to the unknown past to which I was attempting to reconnect. From Sleepy Hollow Cemetery,[20] perhaps, Thoreau will join me?

As a good pedestrian, I stayed to the left hand side of the road as I made my way past the library. In fact, if possible, throughout the day, I would stay to the left in search of dirt shoulders, weedy ditches, lawns of any type or quality, cart paths passing thru orchards, and in dirt covered parking lots … in short, anything to keep my feet and legs from finding the heat and hardness of macadam and cement surfaces. It was a good practical rule of the day. It was a good way to start.

> When I go through a village, my legs ache at the prospect of the hard graveled walk. I go by the tavern with its porch full of gazers, and meet a miss taking a walk or the doctor in his sulky, and for half and hour I feel as strange as if I were in a town in China; but soon I am at home in the wild world again, and my feet rebound from the yielding turf. [21]

In true sauntering mode, my mind wandered as I walked and observed and thought. I thought of the roads of the mid-1800s. They were frequented by carts, carriages, wagons and sleds (in the winter) and were composed of dirt, cobblestone and for short stretches, brick. I turned and looked behind me in hopes of catching a glimpse of the old times, the old road, the old homes, the trees, and the fences. Into the early morning air of Concord, I squinted and closed my mind to the 21st century … it was there; surely, it was there. I

---

[20] Burial grounds for Thoreau as well as other renown of Concord including Louisa May Alcott, Nathaniel Hawthorne and R.W. Emerson.

[21] Henry David Thoreau, *Men of Concord and Some Others as Portrayed in the Journal of Henry David Thoreau*, ed. Francis H. Allen with illustrations by N. C. Wyeth (Boston: Houghton Mifflin, 1936) 183.

even got a sense that we were not alone. Henry? Richard? Is that you?

Just before Thoreau Street, at 255 Main Street,[22] I glanced to my left at the large "yellow" house still within the grasp of the shadows of trees lining the street. At the time, I mentally compared it to our home in Leominster, also yellow with white trim, highlighted in green. I looked for a telltale nightlight but could see none. Henry was not at home.

Reaching Route 2W, I took the left hand fork remaining on Main Street (Route 62W). It was here that I was struck by the appearance yet another large yellow house with white trim and green shutters. I'm sure it stood out because of the yellow color and the similarity with our home. As I would see throughout the day, there would be more yellow homes to come; quite a popular color it is.

Notwithstanding my steps to the left side of the road, they also took with them the moisture of the dew resting on the grassy patches through which I strolled. Soon I could feel the dampness in the uppers of my walking shoes. I hoped they would dry quickly with the appearance of the sun. Surely Thoreau and Fuller did not have the advantages of modern science and industrial design coming through the soles of their feet. I could only imagine the heavy cowhide boots laced high above the ankle to ward off pebbles and twigs. There is nothing "high-tech" about the solution, but Thoreau frequently had trouble tying his laces tightly and securely. Naturally this caused him considerable delays in stopping to retie them. It was not until 1853

[22] The Thoreau family residence was purchased in 1849. It was there that Henry died on May 6, 1862.

that he learned the value of the square knot![23] He would have marveled at the science of Velcro!

Cawww caww caw. Although somewhat different than the pealing bell I had heard a while back, the modern chanticleers of Concord spotted me and sent a greeting from high above. Perhaps I posed a threat? I must admit, a stranger sight they might not have crossed this summer but not a threat by any means. Their screaming sounded louder in the empty morning air. Would they wake tenants of the well-maintained homes of Main Street? No shouts were heard nor did I hear the slamming of windows. "Move on," they seemed to say, "we pardon your trespass."

Thoreau too, was no stranger to these black birds from on high as they faced him where he traveled in and about his hometown. He writes of the crows in *Journal 1*: "Still the crow caws from Nawshawtuct to Anursnuck—as no feeble tradesman nor smith may do—and in all swamps the hum of moskitoes drowns this modern hum of industry."[24] As I am now not far from Nawshawtuct, my pursuers are likely distant relatives of Thoreau's assailants.

Continuing down the street, I was reminded that Thoreau deeply appreciated the magnificent building structures of the town. In *Walking*, he reports that such beauty "never turns in, but forever stands out and erect, keeping watch over the slumberers."[25] Concord, resting in the twilight, gives the aura of a fresh, clean, well-to-do town, its inhabitants proud of their heritage and their place in society and in his-

---

[23] Thoreau, *Men of Concord and Some Others as Portrayed in the Journal of Henry David Thoreau* 98.

[24] Thoreau, *Journal Volume 1: 1837–1844*, 75.22–25. Entry dated "July 11th –39" Two hills located in the town of Concord. Spellings have changed over time, and now it is Nashawtuc Hill and Annursnac Hill.

[25] Thoreau, *Excursions* 188.31–33.

tory. From the street and the sidewalks upon which I quietly strode, fences and front yards were well maintained; homes sported fresh bright painted finishes; lawns and gardens, professionally designed and manicured, reflected a sense of style and fashion.

They were clearly "old homes" but both private and public areas, I noted, remain as well maintained as Thoreau found them to be. Cawww caww caww. In his Journal entry for July 2, 1851, Thoreau wrote, "Many large trees—especially elms about a house are a surer indication of old family distinction & worth—than any evidence of wealth. Any evidence of care bestowed on these trees—secures the traveller's respect as for a nobler husbandry than the raising of corn & potatoes."[26] This surely gives meaning to the old French proverb, *"Plus ça change, plus c'est la méme chose"*—"the more things change, the more they remain the same." I wondered ... how many more things "remain the same?"

Unlike other villages and public ways through which I have passed, there was very little litter on the ground—some but not much.

Along with the cemeteries previously mentioned, I paid special attention to historical markers with dates and events, for they provided clues about what Thoreau may have seen and experienced on his trip. A sign at Woodward Lane indicates that locomotives loaded fuel here at "The Depot" in the mid-1840s when the Fitchburg Railway made its appearance and changed the landscape forever. But in 1842, it was still horses, oxen, carts and wagons.

In no time at all, I reached the banks of the Sudbury River, blanketed in a light covering of early morning fog. There, in the middle of South Bridge, I gave pause for refreshment and a stretch, relieving

---

[26] Thoreau, *Journal Volume 3: 1848–1851*, 284.7–11. Entry dated "July 2nd"

my shoulders of the weighted pack; I was just warming up.

Leaning over the cement railing and gazing to the water below, I encountered a sense of peace and contentment. Most likely, it spread throughout the neighborhood. Minute by minute, the shutters covering the sky began to open and reveal a pastoral riverside scene. Wisps of fog rising from the river flowed gently with the current; kayaks and canoes bobbed gently against the dock; scattered clouds, trees, and flowers of the riverbank lent their image to the mirrored waters of the river.

Thoreau must have found the scene quite the same. A survey of the river and her bridges by Thoreau in June of 1859 indicates that the height of the bridge above the water at South Bridge was just over 6 feet, the depth of the river was 8½ feet and that the span was 114 feet from one bank to the other. I did the math and estimated what was before me. Actually, it hadn't changed much at all.

Across the way, the mirror was suddenly broken by the lunge of a hungry fish seeking an innocent insect gliding over the waters. A rippled wave pattern spread concentrically and gradually to the shoreline. The quiet returned; the river continued its graceful flow to the north. In the distance, perhaps from the heights of Nawshawtuct, I could hear my feathered friends of the sky still debating my presence. Cawww caww caww.

Howard stopped for some pictures. It was a beautiful scene. One side of the bridge, and then the other. Trying to select the right combination of camera setting, light, water, trees, the boathouse, me, reflections in the water, he had much to do and so little time before I decided to shoulder my pack and continue. It was time.

Just up the road, we passed beneath the railroad trestle. And then—another yellow house. I still prefer the Federalist Yellow[27] chosen by Kathleen.

The dim light of dawn had passed and the world was slowly coming to life. An occasional car passed me by, a far cry from the traffic pattern that would emerge by mid-morning. Then again, it was also a far cry from what Thoreau and Fuller experienced. I fought for road space with the moving power of 200 horsepower engines invented years ago by Henry Ford; Thoreau would have passed perhaps a wagon or two each led by a driver and pulled by a team of powerful oxen or draft horses. Their destination may have been to the village blacksmith, to the shoemaker or perhaps to the harness maker. In this, the hay season, one could be sure that it was a well-needed trip and not a trip for social or leisure purposes.

Casually observing the passing land as I sauntered along, I began to notice more and more litter alongside the roadway. I remembered the same finding on many of my training walks taken earlier in the year. Here as I headed out of Concord, I found more of the same: discarded coffee cups and lids from any of several fast food chains, chip bags, cigarette butts, a newspaper insert and an unidentifiable cardboard box. You have to wonder how and why this "stuff" comes to land where it does ....

Recycling containers on the curb couldn't be found in 1842—maybe even 10 years ago. But now, most communities have an active program in place. I am sure Thoreau would approve of these efforts, for even in his day I suspect that in the villages such discarded artifacts might have been found along the roadsides. Active programs

[27] Having changed the tone of yellow a number of times, the final choice when we had the house painted last spring was clearly a wonderful balance. Kathleen calls it Federalist Yellow.

serve to keep the land clean and improve the natural environment for all of us and especially for the wild animals—a real commendable effort. And frequently, I found my footsteps to be on the ultra soft surface of recycled wood chips!

Reaching Route 2, it was devoid of traffic. On a busy midweek afternoon, it becomes a driver's worst nightmare—total gridlock. On this early Saturday morning, I crossed freely, waiting but a few seconds for a couple of speeding cars in flight to the horizon.

The air temperature this morning at departure time was just about 68° F; by now it had risen to the low 70's. Humidity was down and I remained quite comfortable, pausing for a drink of water from my pack as often as I felt a need. I considered carrying a "Camelback" water bladder in my pack so I could drink while continuing to walk, but I felt that, on such a long day, resting was as important as drinking—and thus my decision to carry my water in plastic bottles inside my pack. When thirsty, I stopped. Otherwise, I walked.

A peak at my watch gave the time of 5:42 a.m.; the sun had officially risen! Sunrise is always a special time for me (and for Thoreau) as I strain to catch my first rays coming over the horizon or from behind a tree line. The air is fresh and cool and clean; sound, when there is sound, is that of Nature spilling over the grounds and along the riverbanks.

> What is the pill which will keep us well, serene, contented? Not my or thy great-grandfather's, but our great-grandmother Nature's universal, vegetable, botanic medicines, by which she has kept herself young always, outlived so many old Parrs in her day, and fed her health with their decaying fatness. For my panacea, instead of one of those quack vials of a mixture dipped from Acheron and the Dead Sea, which come out of those long shallow black-schooner looking wagons which we

> sometimes see made to carry bottles, let me have a draught of undiluted morning air. Morning air! [28]

Unfortunately … on the roads of Concord there are too many trees, houses and miscellaneous structures for a direct sighting as the sun crests the horizon. But still, it's the best time of day.

My mind wandered. How much better in the early days was the fuel of transportation? With a team of horses, one paid for feed and pasture; in return, a steady workforce was available for many years ahead. Now in modern times, we have Henry Ford's invention, the automobile, and we need gasoline—not produced here in Massachusetts. I can remember when the price of gasoline was 25¢ per gallon. I must admit, that was years ago; I'm not sure where the oil was coming from … maybe from the Arab states. Now it is up to $61 per barrel and at the pump we pay $2.40 per gallon.[29] Cawwwww Cawwwww.

## *5:47 A.M.—West Concord*

A small bridge lay ahead; the banks were close and overgrown. One could easily pass it by without even noticing. Indeed, it crossed the Assabet and I was entering West Concord. On a previous visit to the town, I had noted that a small shopping strip and a donut shop might be welcome visas for us. An hour had passed since we left Emerson's; the sun was up, and I felt it would be good to stop—have a cup of coffee, a donut, and quiet conversation. And so we did.

---

[28] Henry David Thoreau, *Walden* ed. J. Lyndon Shanley. (Princeton: Princeton UP, 1971) 138.17–28.

[29] By 2007, oil was well over $100 a barrel; gasoline was selling for retail in the range of $3.00–$3.25 per gallon.

It was a short 15-minute break but a valuable one. This was not to be a sprint to the summit; it was an all day journey. We had no fear of rest stops and breaks. By the end of the day, we would be thankful for the conservative approach.

Surely, the attendants could not have been more taken aback as purchases were made and we retired to the patio, which was outfitted with tables and chairs. Howard collected it all on film. It was a perfect morning for eating in the open air. We laughed at their puzzled expressions and sat back to relax for a moment. With his seemingly curious ways, surely villagers had viewed Thoreau with the same sense of bewilderment. Since beginning our trip to Concord almost an hour ago, it was the first time we had to pinch ourselves and take a breath. Indeed, we were really on our way!

At 6:14 a.m., having used the rest facilities, we resumed our walk. I doubt if Thoreau gave the least bit of thought for rest facilities. There were surely plenty of "private" facilities along the way. With the increase in population and the surfeit of homes, it was a major concern of mine as I considered the route.[30]

Passing a quite typical neighborhood of West Concord as we headed to the Westvale section of town, I thought back upon Thoreau's comments that people tend to become slaves to their abodes and accordingly, loose the opportunity to enjoy nature. Well, most of these lawns and yards that I passed need to be mown approximately once a week. Flower gardens must be tended, often on a daily basis. Backyard pools need pumps, filters and cleaning equipment. As for the lawns, I saw no goats and sheep that would do the job most fa-

---

[30] A scan of the route beforehand indicated where I might find public rest facilities and where I might be forced to rely upon the cover of a tree, a clump of trees, or a line of dense bush cover.

mously. Ah, the family lawn mower would do the trick today, but that requires time and—gasoline. And so, it is true, even today we are slaves to our property—and that includes me. I break from my dreams as we neared Westvale. The sign to the right indicated Old Stow Road; it was 6:28 a.m.

Close by the side of the street, a middle-aged man was doing some work in the driveway of his home; I acknowledged him with a pleasant "Good Morning." But, he barely responded; there would be no conversation here. And so, I pushed up the road on the hill—"Old Stow Road."

I paused at the railroad overpass and gazed at the iron rod stretching far and straight into the distance in both directions. To the east, it would reach Concord; to the west, South Acton and points beyond.

Since discovering Thoreau's survey of the Acton/Concord town line which he completed in 1851,[31] I had suspected that this portion of the route might pose a problem in defining the route taken by Thoreau and Fuller. I spent considerable effort in studying this document. In fact, it's not a *document*; it's a work of *art*. Off to the side, in small print, bound between two dotted lines indicating a "lesser road of some type," he had written the words "Old Road to Stow." The message suddenly became clear; while this was once "the road to Stow,"[32] it had become, at least by 1852, an abandoned and little used passageway taken by the railroad bed; his dotted lines stand

---

[31] Henry David Thoreau, Land and Property Surveys: *Acton/Concord Town Line … [Sept. 15, 1851]* The Concord Free Public Library, Special Collections. <http://www.concordlibrary.org/scollect/ Thoreau_Surveys/1.htm>.

[32] Before Acton was incorporated in 1735, Stow was the adjacent town to the west–thus Stow Road.

as a marker for "the old road to Stow." Today one cannot travel that road by automobile much less a horse drawn carriage. But open in July of 1842, it surely provided a clear and viable route of travel to the west and Wachusett.[33]

I thought back on the survey as I continued around the bend. Rather than continuing up the paved road, I dove into the woods at the end of the lane.

Entering the wooded path, I noticed it to be about the width of a car or a carriage; there was a dual set of tracks—just the right size. The base was of dirt and in the center, it was overgrown with grass and small plants; shrubs and small trees were gradually conquering the outer edges. Shady, cool, and quiet; noise from the nearby road was gone. The pathway, for it could hardly be called a road, wound its way deeper and deeper into the forest.

I thought back on what it might have been in Thoreau's time … dirt surface, bumpy tracks of oxen or hoofs of the team of draft horses, the trees close at hand. On the 1830 map of Concord, as well as the 1831 map of adjoining Acton, this is indeed a heavily wooded area parted by a 3 or 4-rod swath from one edge to the other. Today, new roads and construction are closing in on both sides, but it remains a wooded area perhaps protected only by the railway's right of way.

### *6:41 A.M.—Acton*

Around a bend in the path I noticed a granite marker on the side of the "road." The town boundary is somewhere in this vicinity, I thought to myself; might this be a marker for the Acton/Concord

---

[33] On the 8/06/05 walk, I continued up the hill to School Street, on to South Acton and Upper Stow Common by way of Stow Road. On 7/07/06, I walked the following route to Upper Stow Common, to meet the 8/06/05 route.

boundary? Was I about to enter Acton: "Tree City, USA?"[34] Apparently so, and at 6:41 a.m. I was standing with one foot in Concord, the other in Acton; the year was 1842.

Both Thoreau and Fuller comment on the forest, and indeed, this provides a clue to confirm that they passed this way. Fuller wrote that they "soon came to a wood that lies between Concord and Stowe. Here we cut us each a cane; and I thought on farmers, as I passed out of the wood and their green fields smiled upon us."[35] He never gave direct mention to Acton although surely it is Acton that lies between Concord and Stow.[36] Thoreau, on the other hand, makes reference to the fact that at this point of the day, while passing thorough Acton, they were in possession of "stout staves in our hands."[37] There is no explanation as to exactly where they obtained them.

And as for me, I admit to using a walking stick, albeit the modern version crafted of aluminum—along with a multitude of others in a factory somewhere in a far away land. My guess is that Thoreau and Fuller used one each whereas the modern technique is one for each arm. While generations apart, we all recognized the aid that a simple extra appendage provides to the saunterer, the long distance saunterer in particular.

---

[34] Harold R. Phalen, *History of the Town of Acton* (Cambridge: Middlesex Printing, 1954) 147. One derivation of the name Acton is from an Old Saxon form of Ac-Tun, an oak settlement or a village in the woods.

[35] Richard Fuller, "Visit to the Wachusett," *The Thoreau Society Bulletin,* Bulletin 121(Fall 1972) 1–4. Fuller's account ends at Stow as the continued report in another volume has been lost as "Book Second."

[36] Until July 21, 1735 when the town of Acton was incorporated, the town of Concord held that land. At that time this western section of Concord was called Concord Village.

[37] Thoreau, *Excursions* 31.35.

In a small clearing a few yards from the railroad tracks, I stopped and dropped my pack; a felled tree to the side of the path made a fine place to rest for a moment, to have a drink and a snack, to stop and reflect. There I sat, perfectly motionless except for my eyes. A bird peeked into the clearing and continued on its way. Silence. "How things have changed," I thought. A one-time major road of passage from one village to another now reduced to a nondescript overgrown footpath. Most landscapes change with a continuous addition of modern developments or technologies; this one had long passed its once busy life. A breeze stirred and then retreated. Tired trees, fallen trees of yesterday, an overgrown path scared by hoofs and wooden wheels … holding on, hoping against odds … for traffic of any type. Surely, I was a welcome sight, but a mere pedestrian—a far cry from the past. I, a *mere* pedestrian? I looked down the path and thought perhaps, I saw two fellow sojourners turn round the bend and out of sight.

A rumble from the ground came up through my seat secured to the earth. I looked about, recognizing nothing. Louder and louder it came from the north. The ground shook with intense vibration and force; I could feel nature's bench rattle violently beneath me. And suddenly a train shot into view just yards away, powerfully charging eastward toward Concord. The onrushing locomotive moved waves of air; the bushes and the trees genuflected as if in tribute. I stood to closer examine the moving spectacle … and then, as quickly as it had come, it was gone. Silence returned to the wood. I heard a whimper, a whimper of the past. I wondered if this was what Thoreau might have experienced as he saw the railroad invade his domain, nature's domain. It wasn't the steam engine of the early railroad days, but it didn't matter.

> What's the railroad to me?
> I never go to see
> Where it ends.
> It fills a few hollows,
> And makes banks for the swallows,
> It sets the sand a-blowing,
> And the blackberries a-growing,
>
> But I cross it like a cart-path in the woods. I will not have my eyes put out and my ears spoiled by its smoke and steam and hissing.[38]

It was only a short period after his walk through this wood that the rumble would overrun the continual silence of nature. Never again would it be the same. But I could still imagine it. And it was a beautiful moment.

Continuing through the wooded area north of the railroad tracks, I advanced down the path closer and closer to the tracks. Reaching them, I crossed and continued to a condominium development located on Parker Street. As it was originally laid out, the "Road to Stow" passed a bit to the south, but that is now private property.

At 7:30 a.m. on Parker Street, I turned left and headed south toward Stow Lower Common. I eagerly anticipated reaching the Great Road. Be patient. Within minutes, I reached the Independence Road–Parker Street intersection; this was clearly where the Old Road to Stow would have emerged in the 1840s. At last, I was back on the Lancaster Road/Stow Road headed south to the Great Road.

Looking about, I was most disappointed. There were no fields; there were no forests; there was little green to be seen; I saw only house after house after house. My eyes saw no "open country" nor "hop fields;" my nose was not tickled with "the fresh scent of every

---

[38] Thoreau, *Walden* 122.19–27.

field;" my ears heard not "the sound of the mower's rifle." Moving along, I passed Fletcher Corner, where rested at one time a large field where many a baseball game was played as early as the 1850's.[39] To-day—no game, and soon I reached the border and crossed into Maynard.[40]

## *8:05 A.M.—Maynard (Stow)*

Just more houses. Yes, there was the Maynard Country Club and the pristine green rolling fairways, but my imagination was, at that point, too stressed. It was very difficult to turn back the clock and hear the sounds of nature; the ping of a struck golf ball or the whine of a golf cart just didn't do it. I only hoped that better things lie ahead.

I suspected that the "tributary of the Assabet, in the latter town, [Stow]"[41] mentioned in Thoreau's essay, could only be Pratt's Brook. It was scarcely noticeable as I passed, and in an instant, it was in my rear view mirror. But still, it was another clue; it helped confirm my choice of this as the route taken by Thoreau and Fuller.

Perhaps I would find a bit of the old country on Pampositicutt Street, the last roadway that plunged down to Lower Common. Indeed, a swampy area and an orchard were in the distance; I felt better. We were back on the way west.

A busy intersection, with an old cemetery on one corner, stretched before me at the Common area and Route 117 at 8:35 a.m. This might have been called the Bolton Road in times past. But, in

---

[39] Phalen, 147.

[40] Maynard was incorporated from land holdings of Stow and Sudbury in 1891. Following the river to the west, the Lancaster Road went from Acton into Stow.

[41] Thoreau, *Excursions* 31.33–34.

fact, it was more than that. It was the Great Road. Given the traffic and the number of cars in an adjacent parking lot, it would have been quite the same for Thoreau and Fuller. The Great Road was primary passage to reach the western towns of the Commonwealth as well as those in New Hampshire, Vermont, and New York. It was forever busy with carts, carriages, coaches, and livestock. It actually begins in Cambridge and leads westward to Lancaster. Formerly known as The Post Road or Bay Road, it is now commonly known as Route 117. Heading west, we advanced on Upper Stow Common.

It was just after 9:00 a.m., and we decided to take a well-earned break at a local "tavern" opposite the town hall building in Upper Stow Common. Reaching this point of the journey, I was well pleased. While there was nothing significant about Upper Stow Common, it was ten miles from *Bush*. Perhaps for that reason alone, it was a milestone. Sitting on the curb, we enjoyed the brief but well-earned respite, and after a bottle of Gatoraid®and a bag of peanuts, we recommenced our trek.

From the "tavern", it was a long flat haul ahead to Bolton, at least according to the map that's what it looked like. But it was far from boring as we encountered some rather interesting sites along the way. Leaving Stow, we passed a number of fine old homes, well kept over the years, a church, schools, and a number of establishments selling local produce—fruit, vegetables, and flowers. Of course, what great stretch of Americana exists without the grace of Dunkin Donuts®? The franchise sates a number of quests for a caffeine fix, but its disposable cups and lids could fill a number of landfill sites as well. The well-marked papers left a trail up and down the Great Road. For me, the presence of these coffee houses had but one useful amenity: clean restrooms. We used them without shame when nature called.

Gradually, we made our way to a more wide-open country. This was more like it! And while there are modern homes and business structures to be found along the way, the feeling was definitely one of moving in a westerly direction.

### *10:28 A.M.—Bolton*

Around a long sweeping bend in the road was an orchard—a large, working orchard with lines of apple trees, rows of vegetables and mounds of herbs—The Bolton Spring Farm. The apple trees ran in straight lines with colorful ribbons attached, each color marking the variety of apple which each tree bears. The ribbons shifted in the light breeze. I silently slid off the highway and followed a nearby cart path amongst the trees knowing that I would rejoin the road around the bend at the far end of the orchard. A hired hand directed a tractor down the road and into the orchard, winding his way deeper and deeper amongst the trees. The chug of the tractor was all I could hear. Comfortably away from the whine of the usual road noise, I walked slowly in the dusty path enjoying the diversion. I was in no hurry to rejoin the modern Great Road. But finally a patch of pumpkins and squash was before me, and then—the road beyond. I could go no further; the orchard was spent. For now, no more bees, crickets, butterflies, bugs, and off-road smells; no more flowers; no more low hanging boughs bearing soon-to-be sweet red orbs; no more ribbons waving in the wind.

Below on the Great Road, the course did not go so well for Howard. The tractor was towing an active pesticide spray device. And what he thought to be water, as it fell to his windshield, was actually pesticide for the apple trees. A washing would be in order after the trip.

Near Great Brook Farms on the outskirts of Bolton, we reached Great Brook, the site of a memorable encounter by Thoreau and Fuller. Since it is one of only a few place names that are mentioned in the essay, I had eagerly anticipated this encounter. But alas, it would have been more aptly named *Great Disappointment.*

I bound over the guardrail and, hand over hand, crept along the side of the bridge abutment. The banks of the stream were steep and unforgiving; the scene would have been grim had I lost my grip, stumbled, and plunged to the stream below. But I wanted to get as close to Great Brook as possible. Thoreau and Fuller had rested on its banks; I was simply hanging on for dear life.

Perhaps there were once adjoining fields, that provided the farmers a livelihood,[42] but now they were gone, completely overgrown as the water meandered aimlessly from one side of the road to the other. There were no farmlands in sight, no farmers driving their oxen, no neighbor's, not much of anything; just a dark, gnarly, hot forest and swamp. Not a "great brook" by my definition.

Remembering Thoreau's question to "the mower in the adjacent meadow"[43] as to their whereabouts at this point in the journey, I knew that we had reached the outer bounds of Thoreau's geographic map. From this point of the trip, he was heading deeper and deeper into the unknown west.

Continuing down the road, I wandered from one side to the other side; at times I turned deeper into the trees that run parallel to

---

[42] *Bolton Reconnaissance Report*, Massachusetts Heritage Landscape Inventory Program, June 2006. [cited 2007]. <http://www.townofbolton.com>. This was the beginning of the section of Bolton called "Pan." In the late 1700's, Great Brook powered sawmills and gristmills so it was indeed a vibrant locale at the time and certainly with a different appearance.

[43] Thoreau, *Excursions* 32.28.

pavement. But I found not a lot of excitement in there either; it was only a change of scenery. I did find a copy of yesterday's edition of *The Boston Globe*, wrapped neatly in a plastic bag, perhaps lost from the paper carrier passing the news. But then again, maybe it fell from the stagecoach as it rolled westward along the bumpy roadway. I placed it in my pack, soon to be deposited in a rubbish barrel at the Bolton Farms Winery. It was the least I could do in the interest of a clean environment, but I couldn't haul it all out!

I passed the Pan Burying Ground, an old site established in 1822 (East Burying Ground).[44] Moving ahead, I passed another farm stand, and then the landscape returned to one of small markets, businesses, homes and highway. Interstate 495 was within view.

And in itself, that was a joy; for now I was easily within distance of Bolton and the orchards—just about half way to West Sterling. My spirit, and accordingly my face, lit up with happiness. Singing "happy tunes," my step quickened. And my stomach pined for the egg salad sandwich, which I knew, would be set for lunch by Kathleen, my wife. The plan was for our wives to meet us at the orchard for lunch. It was a good time as I strode purposefully under the interstate overpass.

As the hours passed and the sun climbed higher into the sky, I noticed that it was getting a bit warmer. Ahead, at the orchard, I saw "shade" and "rest" so it really didn't matter in the least bit. Passing through Bolton, we stopped just beyond "the blinking light." On the corner, a red wood-clad building rests where formerly stood an old school house. Perhaps it is the one to which Thoreau referred as he

[44] *Bolton Reconnaissance Report*, Massachusetts Heritage Landscape Inventory Program, June 2006. [cited 2007]. <http://www.townofbolton.com>.

wrote:

> The very children in the school we had that morning passed, had gone through her wars, and recited her alarms, ere they had heard of the wars of neighboring Lancaster.[45]

I have no real evidence to support the fact that this might be the exact schoolhouse for by then several had been passed several since leaving Concord. But because of the reference to neighboring Lancaster Village, situated immediately to the west, I always focused upon this particular schoolhouse. I paused and Howard caught me in the lens.

At "the blinking light," I turned left onto Watoquadoc Hill Road. Just a bit farther up the road and we would be at the orchard. At the bottom of the hill, I angled off the road and into the orchard with its soft gentle surface.

### *12:00 P.M.—Nashoba Valley Winery, Bolton*

It was now noon, and at last we had reached the spot chosen for the mid-day break. Kathleen and Taina, Howard's wife, had not yet arrived with lunch.

The winery is situated about a third of the way up Watoquadoc Hill, where Thoreau and Fuller stopped to rest in the early afternoon. It was close enough, and there, beneath a large oak beside the driveway, I lay down my pack, spread a ground cloth, and closed my eyes to wait for their arrival.

> ... and there, on the top of a hill, in the shade of some oaks, near to where a spring bubbled out from a leaden pipe, we rested during the heat of

---

[45] Thoreau, *Excursions* 34.19–22.

the day, reading Virgil, and enjoying the scenery.[46]

I fell asleep for a bit, but my body was still running in fast mode so it wasn't a very long nap. Awake, I was refreshed with newfound energy. I opened my paperback *Walden*, but like Thoreau, my mind traveled elsewhere.[47] I looked off into the distance. The hillsides spread beyond the orchard to the east, green and picturesque. Below our vista, I could see the white church steeple of First Parish of Bolton.

At last our wives arrived and lunch was served. It was a wonderful spread including all my favorites. Unfortunately, I was not as hungry as I thought. I wanted to pack the cooler items for later in the afternoon or perhaps for supper at "the inn," but they would have soured in the heat. I had to pass and take a rain check. Soon it was time to continue. The time was 2:30 p.m., actually, a bit later than I had hoped.

Leaving the parking lot of the winery, I turned left and was back on Watoquadoc Hill Road where I was immediately faced with a steep incline to surmount, for the winery is only at the base of the hill. In no time at all I made the turn on to Old Bay Road and continued up Watoquadoc Hill. I was headed to the highest point on this ridge; one from which Thoreau gained his first close-up view of their destination—Wachusett. But for Howard and me, we were too short; the trees had grown too high along the road to allow a clear sightline. And furthermore, we were prevented from reaching the "top of the hill" by a tall wire fence on which hung signs advertising "private property". I knew exactly where to look for Wachusett, but I could only imagine. My guess is that off to the right in the open meadow a

---

[46] Thoreau, *Excursions* 33.21–25.

[47] Thoreau, *Excursions* 33.34. Reading was not going to calm either of us.

clear view was available—if you wanted to climb the fence.[48] We did not.

My hip seemed to be a bit tight, but as I moved to the soft shoulder, it improved with each step. And once again, I began to feel the mid-afternoon sun beating down upon me. If it hadn't been so warm, I surely would have made tracks to the field off to my left. But no, for the time being, I stayed in the shade of the trees lining the road. They were misshapen old trees that had obviously been in residence for years, their branches arched over the road as if guided by a trellis. I wondered if they might have provided shade for Thoreau and Fuller a few years back.

Over the top and headed into the valley of the Nashoba, I saw a farmer riding a tractor in an adjacent field. A sweet scent of freshly mown hay filled the air, and a cloud of dust rose behind him as he swept the rows of drying hay, churning it so as to complete a good drying before the baler arrived. I remember well my days of haying as a youngster. The scythes used in the hard to reach areas and the sickle bar mower pulled by an old WWII version Jeep, made quick work of large fields. Then the raking began as we prepared the crop for the final step of loading the hay wagon with pitchforks. The most skilled of all was the one riding the load and removing the sheaths of hay from the forks as they were thrust high up to the load. There, the bundle of hay was carefully placed for balance and ease of removal in the barn. It was a hot, sticky job, but at least he got to ride.

Passing the intersection of Old Bay and Wilder Road, I advanced toward the Twin Springs Golf Course. I checked my watch; it was

---

[48] In July 2006, I did just that. In fact, I did better; finding an opening in the security, I drove my car up through the orchard roads to the top. My hunch was quite on the mark; the view was formidable.

3:03 p.m. and I was on the final descent off the hill and just about to enter the village of Lancaster.

And now, the sun seemed beat down upon me more intensely than ever. It was so hot—so very hot, and I sought shade—anywhere I could find it. Nothing had changed over the years; I recalled that Thoreau, coming from Watoquadoc Hill, mentioned the hot valley of the intervale. That's were I was now, and the air was still and motionless and burning. No relief. I looked about to see if perhaps Thoreau and Fuller mocked me from the shade of a leafy bush.

> But we soon learned that there were no *gelidæ valles* into which we had descended, and missing the coolness of the morning air, feared it had become the sun's turn to try his power upon us.[49]

## *3:13 P.M.—Lancaster*

The sign read "Lancaster est. 1653." I passed a shaded cemetery that appeared to be relatively new—Eastwood Cemetery. One thing for sure, it isn't full; there is plenty of open space for future holdings. Wandering into the cemetery that bounds the road, which was now identified as Old Common Road, I read some of the stones; clearly this was a fairly new cemetery. But gradually, as I moved along, it ran into an older section where the markers are nearly 200 years old; research later indicated that this was the Old Common Cemetery opened early in the 18th century. I noticed that the headstones don't specify when the individual had been born, only the year of death and the age. There I found: *Simeon Health, 77 years old, 1844; Mary Cleveland wife of William Cleveland, 35 years old; Joseph Miller, Esq., died 1814, age 66.*

At approximately 3:30 p.m., I sought shelter from the relentless

---

[49] Thoreau, *Excursions* 35.4–8.

heat, not into the woods but to the convenience store at Five Corners intersection just before the bridge that crosses the South Branch of the Nashua River. I dropped my pack; Howard parked the car; and we stood for a minute in the shade of a small tree outside the store. Still too hot! Inside we purchased ice-cold soft drinks that really hit the spot.

About a quarter of a mile to the east of the store, the North and South branches of the Nashua meet. From that junction the river runs north, eventually joining the Concord River and later the larger Merrimack which meets the ocean in Salisbury. So, in fact, Thoreau, Fuller, and I had crossed the lands between the river valleys of the Concord and Nashua Rivers.

The cool air-conditioned store was only a brief reprieve; we couldn't stay forever. And so, back outside, I hefted my pack and plunged headlong into the intervale, the very hot and dry intervale. There was no sense in delaying the inevitable march across the plains.

This area of Lancaster is the area formerly called "the neck" where rich lands of the intervale made for good farming in days gone by. And even today as I looked to either side of the bridge, there were expansive fields of corn, the stalks rising to heights well over my head. Down the road, I saw heat waves rising from the roadbed. It was like walking into a blast furnace. Thoreau had warned me, I have to admit.

> The air lay lifeless between the hills, as in a seething caldron, with no leaf stirring, and instead of the fresh odor of grass and clover, with which we had before been regaled, the dry scent of every herb seemed merely medicinal. Yielding, therefore, to the heat, we strolled into the woods, and along the course of a rivulet, on whose banks we loitered,

> observing at our leisure the products of these new fields.[50]

At the bridge I paused and peered over the side. Even in the middle of summer, the current of the South Branch is quite swift. Off to side, I spotted an old rickety wooden bridge hidden in the camouflage of tired shrubs and trees. Obviously the bridge upon which I stood had only recently replaced the older version. In fact, maintenance of the bridges across the Nashua has always been a problem for the village folks in Lancaster. The floodwaters had a habit of doing nasty things to objects placed in its path. Howard ducked down a side road for a close up of the old bridge and a view of the sign that stands before it as a monument to the past. Indeed, we learned that it was the Atherton Bridge, named for James Atherton, a signer of the petition for incorporation of the town in 1652. It was first erected of steel in 1870.[51] And before that, it would have been a wooden structure.

I continued, seeking shade from somewhere—anywhere along the road. Half way across the "corn flats," I found it as a funny thought struck me: from the movie, *Field of Dreams*, old timer "Shoeless Joe" Jackson and other ball players come forth as ghosts of the past; they come straight out of Ray Kinsella's cornfield to play on the adjacent diamond. Finding a convenient spot, for I did not want to damage the corn, I hid amongst the stalks and had Howard take a picture of me, aka Henry David Thoreau, coming forth from the cornfield. Maybe this wasn't so far fetched after all; I believe the spirit of Henry was indeed with us.

---

[50] Thoreau, *Excursions* 35.15–22.

[51] From the citation printed on the sign located at the foot of the original bridge.

Passing by some local residents at the end of the cornfield, I had the following exchange.

Bob: "How you doing? … Nice out, huh?" Resident: quizzical look of astonishment, nothing said.

Bob: "Nice out, huh?"

Resident: "Yup."

End of conversation. Oh well. I continued toward Lancaster, noticing that homes in this area are set real close to the street; in fact, I could easily see in the windows. While Thoreau heard music coming from some of the homes he passed; I heard the modern day entertainment center, the television, as it blasted away with children's programming.

I didn't see many people out and about; perhaps it was the temperature that drove them inside—inside to the comfort of an environment powered by the air conditioner. I passed a couple of backyard swimming pools, but no one was floating in the water in an effort to escape the heat. Maybe it really was hot out, and everyone was staying inside!

Around the bend, I approached the campus of Atlantic Union College—Bolton Road and Main Street, Lancaster. It was 3:55 p.m. and soon I was on Sterling Road, headed directly to Sterling. In 1842, this as a well traveled route known as the *Mail Route from Westminster to Boston.*[52]

I began to get excited; now I truly sensed the western landscape of Wachusett.[53] I sauntered up Sterling Road and approached the

---

[52] A Town Map from History of Lancaster drawn up in 1795 refers to this as the Post Road or the Old Common Road.

[53] Perhaps I am merely closer to home and familiar territory; in any case, I shout into the recorder, "I can smell it now."

crest of George Hill where a plaque proclaims: "Captives from the Rolandson garrison house passed their first night after the burning of Lancaster by the Indians. 1575 to 1676 Massachusetts Bay Colony Centenary Commission."

The heat was oppressive. I wondered what Thoreau might have been thinking at various points in the course of this journey. Here in Lancaster, I doubt that he was thinking philosophical thoughts. I surmised that both of our subjects were thinking, like me, about getting around the next bend and moving down the road. No other thoughts passed my mind at this time. Was this a test? Was this a rite of passage?

> The traveller must be born again on the road, and earn a passport from the elements, the principal powers that be for him. He shall experience at last that old threat of his mother fulfilled, that he shall be skinned alive. His sores shall gradually deepen themselves that they may heal inwardly, while he gives no rest to the sole of his foot, and at night weariness must be his pillow, that so he may acquire experience against his rainy days.—So was it with us.[54]

The time was 4:03 p.m.; Howard and I paused to rest on a shaded stone fence that ran along the roadside. A lazy gentle breeze stirred the leaves on the trees, perhaps coaxing me onward. Unfortunately it was like hot air from an oven—very oppressive. The water in my canteen was now bath water warm; there was nothing cool and refreshing about taking a drink. But to avoid dehydration, we had no other choice. I tried the Gatorade™. Cold when purchased at Five Points Store, it barely held a chill at this point. "Henry, why didn't

[54] Thoreau, *A Week on the Concord and Merrimack Rivers*, (Princeton: Princeton UP, 1980) 306.23–32.

you just stop here? It looks as good as anything we might find in West Sterling!" I was hot, sweaty, and tired. But as Thoreau and Fuller continued, so too did I.

> —The wise man is restful—never restless or impatient— He each moment abides there where he is, as some walkers actually rest the whole body at each step, while others never relax the muscles of the leg till the accumulated fatigue obliges them to stop short.[55]

The sidewalk was torn asunder, and repairs were being made by men who probably were thankful that this was Saturday—a day to rest. Another demon of the highway now struck; I was forced again to walk on the macadam. And this was fresh macadam which seemed to be "blacker and hotter" than aged road surface.

At 4:27 p.m. I reached the intersection of Sterling Road with Deershorn Road and George Hill Road. There is a possibility that Thoreau took the Deershorn Road route to Redstone Hill Road; that would have taken him straight to Sterling Center. But Sterling Road, also being the more familiar Post Road, also heads, as one might expect, to Sterling. I believe he chose to continue straight ahead along the flatter passage used by the postal carriages.

At this point, we had reached the western regions we had sought since daybreak. Here, the houses are quite far apart. I also found a number of businesses that have located to the commercial zones between towns. Unfortunately, some of them didn't look as if they were doing too well. Several had apparently closed their doors, perhaps overcome by the heat. Around the corner lay Route 62. I kept telling myself that we were "getting there." And then—there was always the

[55] Thoreau, *Journal, Volume 1*, 81.21–26. Entry dated "Sept 17th –39"

proverbial "false summit"—another corner. I crossed the railroad tracks and a large set of regional power lines. Down the hill, over a stream, and I was on Clinton Road. "So this must be Sterling," I thought, and that little stream must be the one of which Thoreau wrote, "we strolled into the woods, and along the course of a rivulet, on whose banks we loitered, observing at our leisure the products of these new fields."[56]

### *4:49 P.M.—Sterling*

On the outskirts of Sterling, just beyond the border crossing from Lancaster, one finds a large ice cream stand set in the back of a sizeable parking lot; this is the home of the Sterling Ice Cream stand. If Thoreau and Fuller could stop and loiter along the banks of a nearby stream, we could also stop for an ice cream break. We had been on the road just over 12 hours. Indeed, I was slowing down but still having fun. At least I said this speaking into the microcassette between huffs and puffs.

It was a longer stop than usual, but the line was long and we had to wait a bit for service. In any case, we set our gear on a picnic table amongst the rest of the patrons and quietly enjoyed our refreshment. At 5:20 p.m. we departed, continuing along Clinton Road or Route 62. I felt real comfortable approaching the cutoff for Route 190; my training walks had taken me to this area several times. My mind wandered, "I can almost see Legate Hill from here; boy, if I just took a right turn, I could be in my own driveway in about an hour!"

But, on second thought, I would rather not pass over Legate Hill. There, one finds so little Nature. Recently, cresting the Hill, I paused

---

[56] Thoreau, *Excursions* 35.19–22.

and sat on a stone fence for a drink from my canteen. I was between houses, in the shade of an old tree, beside a worn and battered shed. That, I imagined, is what it was in former times … in richer times. Indeed, from the top, the view to the west surely includes our Wachusett. But at what cost? What a shame—more roads, more houses, more swimming pools, all in the name of development? As in Thoreau's day, these "improvements, so called, as the building of houses, and the cutting down of the forest, and of all large trees, simply deform the landscape, and make it more and more tame and cheap."[57] Still true today!

And, as Thoreau continued around the big bend into Sterling, so too would I. It was getting along towards late afternoon, and the temperature was already beginning to drop a bit—especially in the shaded areas of the road. It is about this time of day that Thoreau and Fuller stopped to bath their feet in streams that they happened to pass. For me, the ice cream stand was sufficient; I was re-energized and ready for the final trek of the day.

> As we went on our way late in the afternoon, we refreshed ourselves by bathing our feet in every rill that crossed the road, and anon, as we were able to walk in the shadows of the hills,[58] recovered our morning elasticity.[59]

### *5:47 P.M.—Sterling Hillside Cemetery, Sterling*

"About … let's see, one, two … lets see … three … four, five or

[57] Thoreau, *Excursions* 191.6–10.

[58] The alternate route from Lancaster to Sterling is over Redstone Hill. This route, the Clinton Road, skirted the northern flank of Redstone Hill and was the Post Road or the Sterling Road, obtaining its name from a most common use or from the adjacent town toward which it ran! On a sunny day it would have provided shade to the Northeast side.

[59] Thoreau, *Excursions* 35.33–36.2.

six miles to go," I spoke to myself, mentally calculating how many miles I had remaining for the day. I was feeling some excitement; it was all "downhill from here." I reached the Sterling Hillside Cemetery [Oak Hill Cemetery] at 5:47 p.m. and had a short exchange with Howard to whom I said, "a cemetery never looked so good, 'cause I know that up around the bend, and I can see it now, is the old cemetery, called Chocksett Burial Ground, the post office, Route 12 and Sterling Center." Ten minutes later, I saw the statue of Mary's Little Lamb, which greets visitors to the Common. And then from high above: "Bong … Bong … Bong … Bong … Bong … Bong." The hour of six had been struck by the bell of The First Church of Sterling. It was then that I thought back over the long journey for the day and the ringing of five bells by First Parish in Concord. My day was sandwiched between the ringing of two widely separated church bells. God was surely watching over me throughout the day.

In the center, we found that the Pizza Parlor was still open; a large pie would do nicely and we waited outside. There we encountered a local patron on a run to the pizza shop, but learning of our endeavors of the day, he was more interested in talking hiking and outside lore than pursuing the pizza. Unfortunately "hot pizzas" become "cold" pizzas when not transported home quickly, so off he went when his number was called.

Minutes later, our pie was "up." Hungry and tired, we made short work of the hot steaming pizza. The sooner we got back on the road, the sooner we would arrive at the inn. It was 6:30 p.m. and we only had about 3 miles to go.

The route from Sterling took us along yet another portion of the Old Mail Road to Westminster. Today, it is Route 62. As I noticed in Concord earlier in the day, yellow houses seem once again to proliferate the village scene. The sun ahead of me was slowly sinking into the trees. I figured that perhaps in an hour and a half or so it would set for the evening. As the journey continued, shadows from the trees grew longer with each passing minute.

From the center of town, it's but a short distance to Fitch's Hill and the gray cement structures supporting the ribbon of interstate roadway overhead. "Clink, clink, clink" sounded my poles as I set a brisk and steady pace. As I passed under the overpass, morning doves were heard bedding down for the night: "Coooo cooooo." I felt real confident striding up the road, driving with each push of the poles; "we're gonna make it, gonna make it hon," I said, talking to Kathleen, present only in my thoughts. I noticed a slight blister on the thumb of my right hand where I had been grasping the cork handle of the hiking pole. Nothing major, that's for sure.

At 7:04 p.m. we left Route 62 and turned right onto Beamon Road. I estimated that it would be another 45 minutes or an hour before dusk. We continued along Beamon all the way to the Stillwater River in West Sterling.

### *7:21 P.M.—West Sterling*

There is no marker announcing the bounds of the village, but upon crossing the Wilder Road intersection, I was firmly convinced that I had reached what Thoreau had called "the western part of the town"—the village of West Sterling. Here, a close-up view of Little Wachusett was before me, and Wachusett stood just behind the trees. The grade of Beamon Road was gentle and downward. That was a relief; at this point in the day, my feet were dog-tired.

In the fall of 2004, as I searched for town maps and other indications of roadways that might have existed in the mid-19th century I placed a phone call to the Sterling Historical Society. David Gibbs, the curator, answered the phone. As I described my intent, he was only too happy to help. His excitement stretched through the phone line as he introduced me to the Milton Buss House and Tavern. Familiar with Thoreau's "walk," it was his belief that Thoreau and Fuller had spent the first night at the Buss Inn.

Visiting the site with David two weeks later, I got a good feeling about this location; I had almost enough evidence to agree with him. The property, now overgrown with small trees and vines, lies just across the street from the Gibbs' family home in West Sterling. In the middle of the tangled overgrowth, two deep cellar holes of the old structure are all that remain. I stood quietly and listened for the telltale sign. Straining my ears, I heard it. From across the road came the rush of the Stillwater River. Crossing the road to the river's edge, an old broken and weathered dam could be seen just upstream. "David, when I make this walk, I'll be back."

Passing the Sterling Rod and Gun Club site, Howard shot on up the road to the Gibbs' house, which I described for him; the first night's lodging was at last in sight—the Buss Inn and Tavern. Over the ping, ping of my poles, I heard the voices of young men at play somewhere in the darkening dusk of the day. Five minutes later, I strode onto the Gibbs' property where there were three, hard at play in the yard with a plastic bat and waffle ball: the Gibbs' sons and friend! And thus it was at 8:15 p.m., exactly 15½ hours since leaving *Bush*, we arrived at our first night's destination: West Sterling.

Today, West Sterling is a collection of homes that rests at the intersection of Beamon Road and Redemption Rock Road–Route 31, approximately 4 miles from the center of Sterling. I found no commercial establishment in the area, simply homes built on small lots cut into the dense forest. A quiet residential urban community is a fair description today while in 1842, it was alive with activities driven by the flowing river: the saw mill, the grist mill, the dam, and just as importantly, the tavern, which most likely served as a rest stop along the Westminster to Boston Mail Road. Winding southward along side the Stillwater River, the Mail Road reached this point and turned in an easterly direction toward Sterling Village and Lancaster,[60] leaving the river to plot her own course south to join with the North Branch of the Nashua River in Lancaster.

The mills are now gone as is the tavern erected circa 1820 and formerly open for business as the Milton Buss House and Tavern.[61] What remains are the babbling waters of the river, the broken structure of the mill dam, the foundation and cellar hole of the tavern, and my "tavern for the night", the lawn of Susan and David Gibbs. Thoreau writes: "there was already a certain western look about this place, a smell of pines and roar of water, recently confined by dams ...."[62] No doubt, this was the place.

As if a secret signal had been given, Susan and David suddenly and unexpectedly appeared from around the side of the house. They eagerly greeted us with open arms. Susan, much concerned for our well being, had spring water close at hand. It was a welcome offering, and I eagerly gulped the cold refreshment. David, the historian at heart and quite familiar with Thoreau's walk, was eager to talk of the adventure and our plans for continuing in the morning. He retrieved

---

[60] *Atlas of Worcester County,* 1830 Survey of Sterling by Moses Sawyer, (Pendleton's Lithography, Boston, 1830).

[61] Inventory Form continuation Sheet, Historical Narrative for *Sterling, Pottery Village,* Massachusetts Historical Commission, Massachusetts Archives. Copy held by Sterling Historical Society.

[62] Thoreau, *Excursions* 36.4–7.

a copy of an old edition of *Excursions* and we exchanged stories. With the sun quickly settling below the tree line, darkness was fast approaching, as were the mosquitoes. And so David and Susan left us to set the tent and prepare for the night. "Come on inside, when you're finished. Wash up and have something to eat."

A long day for Howard, his battery was fast approaching depletion. His work for the day complete, he packed the car and headed home, just a short 5-mile trip away. Before his departure, I scribbled a note to Kathleen. "All is well; we're going to make it!"

From the lawn and my tent, the lights from inside the house gave me a warm feeling. I spread my gear in the tent; I felt tired but very much in a place I was supposed to be at this time. Everything arranged for the night, I left the tent to meet with my hosts.

The house struck me as "old" as soon as I stepped into the foyer, and indeed it is. Constructed circa 1835, it represents one of the older homes in the "village" of West Sterling. The wide board, hardwood floors creaked as if to welcome me; surely they had heard talk of the impending arrival of sojourners from Concord. I noticed the low hanging ceilings as I followed David, winding our way to the family room in the back of the home. For Thoreau and Fuller, the inn and tavern, across the road, must have provided similar comfort.

It was well beyond my normal suppertime, and still filled with pizza, I declined the offer of an evening meal. Susan had a feast of Indian cuisine prepared, and I could only think of the "Swedish inn quote" as Thoreau remembered his evening at the Buss Tavern. For Thoreau, perhaps it was a humorous throwaway line, or perhaps not. For me, with no disrespect to the hostess, on this occasion, it was not: "You will find at Trolhate excellent bread, meat, and wine, provided you bring them with you …."[63] I was more interested in washing up and taking a load from my feet. The company was extraordinarily pleasant. Stepping from the 19th century to the 21st century, we enjoyed quiet conversation in overstuffed chairs while the television broadcast of a ballgame droned in the background. I imagine the pleasantries that I experienced at "the inn" were much the same as those experienced by Thoreau many years ago.

And then, it was time to retire. My day was done; I needed sleep for tomorrow's trip up the mountain.

Back in the tent, I quickly found the comfort of my sleeping bag. The temperature was mild, but given the excitement of the occasion and the fact that I don't normally sleep on a mat, in a tent, on the lawn of an acquaintance, beside a highway replete with fast moving automobiles, sleep did not come easily.

Just after midnight, the highway noise ceased and the air got real quiet, but the longer I was in the sleeping bag, the more my body began to ache—muscle aches. Every "bone in my body" felt the pain! I focused on the panorama overhead. The stars were bright, especially Cygnus the Swan, which was straight overhead and gradually flew to the west as the night wore on. Temperatures were in the low 60's;[64] there was little if any wind and no precipitation; I don't know whether it ever got into the 50's or not. It really didn't matter for the tent and the sleeping bag provided all I needed. I strained my ears but could not hear the "murmuring of water" from the Stillwater River across

---

[63] Thoreau, *Excursions* 36.26–28. This phrase originally came from a book by Thomas Thomson, *Travels in Sweden During the Autumn of 1812*.

[64] The high yesterday and today was 82° F. The low was 65° F. last night and it would be 62° F. tonight (probably a bit cooler on the mountain. On Sunday, coming off the mountain and returning home, the temperature reached 87° F.

the road. Having heard its roar in the autumn from this very spot, I supposed the dry summer had taken its toll on the volume of water between the banks. The dark and the quiet of the night soon came and I was fast asleep.

## *7:40 A.M. August 7, 2005—West Sterling*

Cawwww, Cawwwww. Had the crows of Nawshawtuct and Anursnuck tracked me in the night to send me on my way from yet another river?

Howard's presence startled me; I peered from the tent and there was his car; inside, he patiently awaited my return to life. With a night of broken sleep, I awoke later than planned. Unlike Thoreau, I would not leave for the mountain "in the grey twilight."[65] The sun pierced the haze of the cool, early morning air, giving a charge to this tired sojourner. Even the crows were awake; clearly it was time to rise.

No one appeared from within the "inn," although one of the boy's friends had stayed the night and his mother arrived to retrieve him. And in turn, the eldest son had stayed at a friend's home for the night; he too returned about the time I was stirring. Other than that, traffic was sparse: only the sound of the crows from afar and the "wheeet whew wheeeet whew" of an unknown bird.

Before I hoisted my pack and began this leg of the journey, it was important that we briefly explore the site of the Buss Tavern, just across the street. It is state owned property—it's future unclear. While it could be developed, I believe it should be held for historical and archeological purposes. To exactly replicate Thoreau's walk, I thought about setting up my tent on the grounds of the tavern, but it

---

[65] Thoreau, *Excursions* 37.3.

was strewn with far too many branches, trees and rocks to make a reasonable campsite. There is a significant amount of dense growth surrounding the tree-covered site; it screens the passerby from the old and crumbling cellar hole within. Once penetrating the screen, the site opens reasonably well for easy viewing. The foundation and cellar hole of both the barn and the inn remain in a dilapidated state. The cellar hole is, at this point in time, about 6 feet deep. What lies below the base is a mystery. Using the Gibbs' back lawn was indeed an excellent choice.

Following the photo op at the *Inn*, I crossed Route 31, also known as Redemption Rock Road, to wash in the south flowing Stillwater. I took off my hat and shirt, damp from the previous day's walk, and splashed them in the water. I washed my hands and face — perhaps "splashed" is a better description—in the cold sparkling water. Leaning across the broken, wooden beams that once formed a passable bridge, I turned to face the sun and the warm rays that penetrated the green canopy. If only I might stay a while. But I still had miles to go.

So refreshing it was to dunk my hat, to rinse my t-shirt, and then to put them back on. As the morning warmed on the road, they would quickly dry. In any case, it was an invigorating way to start the day.

Like Thoreau, my departure from West Sterling was alone, and like Thoreau, it was "with a kind of regret"[66] that I bid adieu to my hosts, the Gibbs—excellent people, a real nice family—and continued my journey.

Instantly, I noticed that the road ahead had already taken a turn

---

[66] Thoreau, *Excursions* 37.5–6.

"upward" as in seeking higher elevations. From West Sterling, the road winds decidedly uphill, gradually at first but definitely uphill. Early this Sunday morning, a biker passed me coming off the hills ahead, and he went speeding out of sight behind me.

And at the same time, I noticed that there are only a few homes along this stretch of road. My passage was, in simple terms, through a thick, deep forest reflected in brilliant green, compliments of a bright morning sun which had made its presence a factor in the day's weather pattern.

As I continued, I reflected on yesterday's journey … happy to have made the 28-mile distance, a record for me, proud of what we are doing and to be going where we are going. And … all with little or no physical pain in my feet, legs, ankles, or my back. Oh, I felt them for sure, but nothing problematic. I thought of the intervale in Lancaster; for sure that was the most difficult portion of the trip. Twenty miles is the distance classified as the breaking point in a marathon. In fact, that was just about when I hit Lancaster and the intervale. I guess you might say I bumped the wall; didn't break it—just a bump. Twenty-eight miles … a pretty good day's trek. For today, conversely, I shall plod up the road a mere six miles and leave the balance of the day for rest on the mountaintop.

A dead garter snake lay on the shoulder of the road, and my wandering mind returned to the task at hand. Actually, I hadn't seen much road-kill on the trip; just snakes—no skunks, no squirrels, no raccoons—just snakes. I passed a sign that clarifies ownership of this land: Metropolitan District Commission. Fishing, boating, and cross-country skiing are authorized. Yet there will be "no camping, no fires, no skating, no dogs, no horses, no cars, no dumping, no alcohol, no four wheeled vehicles, no boating, no speed boats and no bikes."

Environmental protection! Thoreau would approve, obviously in order to preserve the wild. As a sojourner, I guess I'm authorized. I continue along the road into the Wachusett Area Watershed.

### *9:33 A.M.—East Princeton*

The road way was getting steeper as I approached East Princeton; I checked my cadence into the speaker of the microcasette as I wonder how fast I am chugging up this hill. Here's what I heard: "Chunka-ka-chunk, chunka-ka-chunk, chunka-ka-chunk, chunka-ka-chunk," as I entertained myself. I declared that I was moving up the hill at a blistering pace. Oh the simple things one does for amusement while on the road.

Then, I noticed the ravine—very steep and very deep below the trees to my left. This was no mere gully, no ditch or drain, no mere riverbed at the side of the road. A canyon or chasm might well be the best words to describe this descent to the waters below.[67] I thought about descending, but it was far too perilous for this day's walk. I squinted through the trees and used my eyeglass. Indeed, as Thoreau had indicated, the Stillwater roared below as it made its way amongst the rocks and the trees.

> Our road lay along the course of the Stillwater, which was brawling at the bottom of a deep ravine, filled with pines and rocks, tumbling fresh from the mountains, so soon, alas! to commence its career of usefulness.[68]

And around the bend I walked. Just like that, I was in the center of downtown East Princeton.

---

[67] Topographic maps indicate that from the roadside, the Stillwater can be found 70 to 80 feet lower in elevation after a run of only .07 mile. Indeed, it is steep!

[68] Thoreau, *Excursions* 37.8–12.

Another yellow house greeted me at the portal to the small village. And there I encountered an elderly gentleman tending a small garden of tomatoes by the side of his house, just a few steps from the roadside.

"Morning—how you doin'?" I asked as I reached the property.

Actually, it wasn't a large front yard by any standard; it sat pretty much right on the road. The tall gentleman with silver hair and a slow stooped gait was startled, giving his full concentration to life in the garden. He stood straight as if to gauge the sight was before him.

"Good Morning," he replied.

We introduced ourselves—his name: Bob Halloran, a long-time resident of East Princeton. His hospitality and pleasantness warmed my heart and I removed the pack for a rest. I thought he must have been waiting for me. We talked and he offered a tomato—freshly picked from the vine—and water from his garden hose as well. I drank from the hose and wrapped the tomato for a snack. We talked some more … his family, wife and kids, the schools of today, discipline, the benefits of natural fertilizers, motorcycles, roads and expansion, music and vaudeville, a monument to the heroes of 9/11 soon to be built on the corner. It was hard to break away; one final pull from the end of the hose. Real nice guy; I shall have to return. Good conversation with a good person on the route. My thoughts turned to my journey; I was wondering as to the whereabouts of Howard, not having seen him for a good amount of time.

At 10:00 a.m. the sun was just warming things up on the road. "Woof, woof" two dogs barked by the kitchen door announcing a passing stranger to anyone who would listen. I passed quickly, my mind still on the nice conversation and visit I just had with a complete stranger. I'll definitely have to stop in and visit sometime.

But we were on the move again as I quickly approached the town garage. Just beyond, at the convenience store, I paused for my first real close look at the summit.

"Man, oh man, man", I sputtered. "I don't know what to think." We were so close, so close. I could scarcely believe that I was actually closing in on my destination.

It was 10:07 a.m. and I finally caught a glimpse of Howard at the intersection of Routes 31, 140, and Beamon Road. He had driven to the bottom of the ravine for a photo op. I waved him down and we stopped to rest. Thoreau had found raspberries. But a raspberry-flavored health-bar and the "Halloran-tomato" were the closest I would come to raspberries beside the road; I drank spring water—from the bottle provided by Susan Gibbs. Somewhere there were berries, and for certain, the Stillwater is still fed by waters that leak from the hills. As we rested on the grass by the side of the road, I looked up ahead on Beamon Road; the slope of the terrain continued to be "uphill."

I was soon walking on the road, deep within a thick rich green forest. I envisioned what it must have been like years ago … a carriage road with stone fences and old weathered trees, which marked boundaries of the landowners nearby. I noticed newer homes piercing the landscape, but the square cut architecturally pure fences gave away their secrets. This was no rustic house of old, I knew. From whence did the power lines grow? From vines of the old forest? And the backyard swimming pools surely came from spring driven frog ponds of old. Automobiles, two or three per household, are probably just the equivalent of the large wheeled carriages and the wagons of yesteryear. If possible, the forests and landscape would have staged a mutiny at the carnage spilled in the name of progress.

I closed my eyes to the day and resurrected, as best I could, the past; I turned and saw a team of oxen obediently pulling a cart of hay up the hill, perhaps to the big red barn just round the bend ahead. The driver, dressed for work in his long-sleeved blouse and sporting a wide brimmed hat that protected him from the strong sunshine of the day, quietly followed step by step. The team knew the way. A dog followed behind. Billowing clouds gathered in the distance, reminding the farmer that he must continue. Hay, wet with rain, cannot go to the loft.

Just beyond 161 Beamon Road, I spotted an old cemetery—Parker Cemetery—surely one of the smallest plots I have ever encountered. I climbed the short embankment and entered. With only 30–40 individual plots in this cemetery of about 40' by 100' in area, I completed my walk through in just a few minutes. The uneven yard was well manicured and tended. Cawwww Cawwww. Headstones are dated in the 1800's. I spotted one with the name Lucy Keyes.[69] I was amazed to see the name, only to realize later that "the Lucy Keyes" for which the name has become best known, lived in the mid-1700s. In any case, I read the headstones down the line; these were the settlers that inhabited the lands of which Thoreau was most curious. A real tragedy must have occurred in the Ephreham and Sally Keyes family; Sons Joseph and Ebenezer both died in February of 1810—Joseph on the 24th at the age of 2 years, 2 months; Ebenezer on the 28th at the age of 4 years, 9 months. With all due respect, I had to laugh at the inscription on one headstone; it reads: "Novena Wheeler,

---

[69] *The Legend of Lucy Keys.* On April 14, 1755, a child named Lucy, "aged four years and eight months, attempting as was supposed, to follow her sisters, who had gone to Wachusett pond, about a mile distant, and having nothing but marked trees to guide her, wandered out of her way in the woods, and was never heard of afterwards." <http://www.lucykeyes.com/lucy/legend/lucy_disappears.shtml>

died in 1969, 92 years, 5 months, 14 days." My thought was that they sure were trying to squeeze all the life out of her that they might.

The road continued to climb and I reached Hobbs Road at 10:45 a.m. I marveled at the stone fences on either side of the road; surely these fences have been there for years and years. Replete with generations of moss and lichens, overgrown with bushes and trees, the fences retain their strength, holding memories of a purpose served nobly. An opening indicates that a calamity of some type struck years back. Like the mystery of the Keyes Family, it's an unknown story of why and how the carefully laid stones now find themselves at rest several meters from their brothers. This land, all of it, is a necropolis holding more untold stories than history books will ever tell.

The forest is decidedly hardwood—maples, oaks, and ash. I passed a brook, bubbling from the highlands set before me; later today, its waters will flash down the ravine of the Stillwater. I envisioned yet another carriage passing between the stone fences on either side of the road.

A sign for a missing feline caught my attention as it waved from a power line pole; a train rumbled in the distance although I was not sure of its origin.[70] And then, the drone of a plane overhead—most likely a small one as it circled the summit.

At 11:00 a.m. I had reached the intersection of Wilson Road and Beamon Road at the crest of the long hill that I had been climbing. Having wrestled with the uphill climb since leaving West Sterling, I welcomed the brief downhill stretch to Myrick Road.

---

[70] Passing about 4 miles away, the locomotive was running on the Providence and Worcester Railroad Company line. An interstate freight carrier, it runs between Gardner, Massachusetts and Worcester, Massachusetts, passing through the towns of Hubbardston, Princeton, and Holden. <http://www.pwrr.com>

At last, at the T-intersection of Beamon and Myrick, I reached Thoreau's "base of the mountain."[71] Beyond the swamp that stretched before me, I saw the profile of Wachusett. I paused and enjoyed the quiet. From the swamp to the summit, it was the only distance that remained. An osprey took wing, temporarily interrupting the stillness. And then, the silence returned. One final push was all it would take. And so, I turned to continue and headed uphill once again. This time there was no doubt; I was climbing the mountain.

I continued walking amidst 19th century artifacts. I strolled uphill towards Gregory Road, the final passageway leading to the Wachusett Mountain State Reservation. The ever-present gray stone fences marked the limits of the pastures and fields on either side of the road. The rich emerald green trees welcomed me, providing shade from the hot sun. Pastures extended beyond the fence on one side while a small brook, starved of water at this time of year, gently flowed toward the lowlands and the swamp at the base of the mountain. This, the East Wachusett Brook, will soon find the Stillwater, the Nashua, and eventually the Atlantic. A large garden appeared abruptly on the hillside in the middle of a field spotted with stones that never made the fence. Small green plants huddle close to the ground, protected by blue protective cups; clearly they are seedlings set for harvest in a few years. It's a "natural garden;" it has not felt the power of the tractor or the harrow. My guess is that it was planted and tended by hand, very carefully and very lovingly. I *see* the farmer hard at work carefully tending his planting, on the far side of

---

[71] Thoreau, *Excursions* 37.6–7. From the site of the Buss Tavern, this point stands at 4.16 miles along the road (3.16 miles on a direct line). Thoreau stated that the tavern was but 4 miles to the base of the mountain. The elevation profile from the tavern to the summit gives one a distinct impression that, if there is an easily definable "base," this swamp, from which one can view the summit, is it.

the plot. In fact, it is a sizeable plot perhaps 40 yards by 100 yards. Across the way, pear trees thrive with fruit hanging, still maturing for the harvest soon to come. The fruit has been bagged on the trees to protect it from insects and other natural predators.

My eyes *saw* this … and more from yesteryear. Wood, to provide fuel for the hearth this winter coming, was stacked beside a small shed. The narrow road, barely wide enough for passage of two carriages side by side, continued up and up and up. A family of wild turkeys moved silently beyond the stone fence that bordered the road. Catching sight of me, the larger bird signaled all to immediately stop in their tracks.

Returning to the moment, I moved onward only after pausing to catch my breath and to study the terrain both above and below. I looked skyward through the towering maples and oaks. The stiff metal communication towers, resting as guards on the summit, were no longer visible—a sure sign that I was closing in at last. And then, the capstone on the moment, from the adjacent meadow: "the fresh odor of grass and clover, with which we had before been regaled …."[72] It almost made me stop, sit down in the shade, and drink it all in. But on this day, another place beckoned and I was anxious to reach it.

Finally, at 11:31 a.m., this part of the climb concluded at the junction of Gregory Road and Mountain Road where rests a small parking lot for the Wachusett Mountain State Reservation. But, perhaps more significant, I looked about and found myself in the midst of a large maple stand! Two old gnarly maples in particular stood out from the rest. Their expansive girth, their uneven layers of thick crusty bark, and their bent and withered limbs revealed the secret of

[72] Thoreau, *Excursions* 35.16–18.

their age; they stood perhaps a bit lower to the ground and not as large at the girth as when two strangers from the east passed years ago. Scars of the auger, some barely visible, unearthed stories of the past. But come early spring each year, these trees still feel the drill bit of the sugar harvest.

> In due time we began to ascend the mountain, passing, first, through a grand sugar maple wood, which bore the marks of the auger, then a denser forest, which gradually became dwarfed, till there were no trees whatever.[73]

The well-defined smell of the sugarhouse teased my nose; from my early days on the farm in Vermont, I remembered it well. Tapping the trees, gathering the sap, the 24–7 boils, testing the dark thick syrup as it neared completion, and the ultimate taste test, peeling thin strips of hardened sugar from hard packed snow in the church basement at the end of the season; it all came back as I thought of these trees and their history. As Howard pulled into the trailhead parking lot, I came back in time.

I dropped my bag. The entrance to the State Reservation had finally been reached. We stood before the Mountain House Trail, formerly the Old Coast Survey Road. Aside from the Old Indian Trail, this trail is perhaps one of the first recognized trails to the summit. The earliest records of this trail are found on documents dated 1833. At that time, the path to the top of the mountain was hardly traceable; it had been used but a few times by local residents

---

[73] Thoreau, *Excursions* 37.27–31. The section of the walk where Gregory Road intersects Mountain Road and enters the property of the State Reservation is populated with many very old Sugar Maples. While Thoreau reaches the summit by the end of this short sentence, it is still a mile to the summit from the grove of maples!

and also by surveyor Simeon Borden in 1833.[74] With such a paucity of traffic, it was wild and natural in its growth patterns.

Lunch was served from the back of the "carriage." I quietly gazed at the maples and found them to be yet another link to the past, a link to the time of Thoreau's walk, a link to the beginnings of this country and before that, to the real natives of this great land.

Out of the car for the first time in two days, this was Howard's day in the sun, quite literally. Howard would walk the final mile of Thoreau's trip. We rearranged our gear and made preparations for the final leg to the summit. Everything was packed for the next 12 hours—tent, sleeping bag, pad, stove, food, and plenty of water.

### *12:23 P.M.—Wachusett Mountain, Princeton*

Deep into the dense hardwoods, the trail winds steeply over large rocks some of which were slippery with moss and moisture from mountain runoff. On the other hand, there was no need for speed. It was only 1:00 p.m. and we had the balance of the day before us with no appointments. And so, we alternated climbing with resting and drinking.

Off to the side of the trail, tell tale signs of the pileated woodpecker were most obvious—large oval shaped holes in the trees with a base littered with chainsaw sized chips. This, being a mature forest, is an excellent environment for them to live and to raise their families.

Higher up the Mountain House Trail, where it merges with the Jack Frost Trail, I had, many times in the past, looked back over the terrain and imagined carriages, led by strong surefooted teams of horses, slowly and carefully making their way upward. The trees and

---

[74] Warren M. Sinclair, *Wachusett Gatherings from Then and When* (Salem, Massachusetts: Higginson Book, 1996) 14.

undergrowth beside the trail seemed to lean inward to form an arch through which the visitors would emerge to the upper region of the mountain. It was as if through this royal arbor, they might parade onward to the beauty of the summit just ahead. On this day, Howard and I, along with Thoreau and Fuller, were pioneers from the low-lands, taking part in the parade.

And then, we were there. The lower parking lot and a final climb over the flat rocks that stretch out on the southern ridge led us up the final 25 yards to the summit. I stood atop the stubby cement post with the compass rose for the obligatory photo op. The time was 1:25 p.m.

I had been walking in silence and solitude for the better part of two days when we reached the summit. Quickly the mood and the spirit of my walk with Thoreau came to a halt. As Dorothy said in the 1939 classic movie *The Wizard of Oz*, "Toto, I've a feeling we're not in Kansas anymore." I too, knew that we were now in a different place. On the summit grounds, there were, before us, approximately 75 to 100 people engaged in a number of summertime activities: kite flying, picnicking, conversing, walking, eating, surveying the grounds, gazing to the horizon seeking to recognize monuments of the valleys beyond, riding bikes and scooters, and reading, and writing, and napping. Generally, there was quite a buzz of activity. Some had hiked to the summit, but most, judging from the number of cars parked in the lot, had driven. So many people on the mountain—it is probably the way Thoreau envisioned it ... some day. Or ... perhaps not.

But, having visited the summit a countless number of times in the past, this sight came as no real surprise to me. In fact, it was rather typical for a warm summer day on the mountain. I had left quiet peacefulness on the road below knowing that it would not reappear until dusk, when the sun set to the west and the guests departed down the road. That calm will then flourish through the night and until the valleys below awaken at dawn tomorrow. Definitely, it was a far cry from what Thoreau and Fuller found on their ascent in 1842.

> It is but nineteen hundred feet above the village of Princeton, and three thousand above the level of the sea; but by this slight elevation, it is infinitely removed from the plain, and when we reached it, we felt a sense of remoteness, as if we had traveled into distant regions, to Arabia Petrea, or the farthest east.[75]

No such remoteness did I experience during the afternoon of the 7th day of August 2005.

Having reached the summit, I walked to the side of the trail just beyond the fire-watchtower and there I dropped my pack near a dense growth of high bush blueberries. Straddling the path, I found the tiny spines of the bush to be full and heavy with fruit. They would serve me well later.

Since July 1842, there have been many changes on the summit, and to be sure, they all display the fingerprint of humanity. The Summit Hotels are gone, but in their place are the U.S. Army Corps of Engineers radio relay antenna towers, the ranger's watchtower, paved parking lots and roads, lookout platforms, picnic areas, ski lifts, and a stone memorial dedicated to the memory of the U.S. Army 10th Mountain Division.[76] But, if one can overlook these modern additions, the summit is probably about the same as it was when Thoreau and Fuller reached it.

My layman's survey of the topmost summit area resulted in the

---

[75] Thoreau, *Excursions* 37.32–38.1.

[76] During WW II, this storied division trained on Mt. Wachusett.

following: a clear, rocky, rounded cap of elliptical shape which runs east to west for approximately 80 paces, and north to south for approximately 50 paces—an area of just about .64 acres. Beyond the boundary of the ellipse, the ground drops sharply to an area covered with thick shrubs and small trees. Compare this with what Thoreau observed.

> The summit consists of a few acres, destitute of trees, covered with bare rocks, interspersed with blueberry bushes, raspberries, gooseberries, strawberries, moss, and a fine wiry grass. The common yellow lily, and dwarf cornel, grow abundantly in the crevices of the rocks. This clear space, which is gently rounded, is bounded a few feet lower by a thick shrubbery of oaks, with maples, aspens, beeches, cherries ...."[77]

I found that if one looks, it is still there. Indeed, the vegetation has been pushed aside, but traffic will tend to do that. The remainder? Pretty much the same. Really, it is. Work at it in your mind; it's there.

So there is some change on the summit, and perhaps that should be expected after 160 years, especially when I think of both the enjoyment and the pleasure that the mountain now provides to its visitors. Such accessible woodlands represent a treasure to be shared by all. I have to believe that Thoreau would be pleased.

Shortly before 3 p.m., Howard was ready to descend. It had been a long two days for him, and he was anxious to return home for the evening. We gathered his photographic gear and walked to the Mountain House Trail. I watched as he made his way slowly over the rocky trail, downward, around the bend and gone .... I was now

[77] Thoreau, *Excursions* 38.4–15.

"alone" with Henry and Richard on Mount Wachusett, and of course with a hundred other guests—for now.

### *3:00 P.M.—The Summit Wait*

I wandered back to the sunny spot beside the blueberry bushes where I had left my pack. There I sat and pondered my options for the balance of the day. Usually my trips to the summit involve a short turn around, never lasting more than 30 minutes or so, depending upon the situation and whom I might meet. This visit was decidedly different. I had the next 18 to 20 hours to pass at my leisure. To get started in the tradition of Thoreau, I would first pick some berries for tomorrow morning's breakfast. And while this bush was close at hand, a reasonable search of the area indicated that the blueberry plant has survived for the last 160 years on the summit—probably longer. I wondered if Thoreau had eaten from this very bush.

For the rest of the time, there was reading; writing, people watching, bird watching, sleeping, talking, and of course, thinking.

I must admit that my biggest worry about this trip was staying on the summit for the night. Knowing that the Reservation generally frowns upon such endeavors, I was concerned that I would be discovered and escorted off the mountain. And then, the effort into which I was now so heavily invested would be tarnished and incomplete. I wondered, "are the park rangers really active in their patrols and do they patrol the summit at night? I know they don't officially sanction overnight visits, so what should be my best approach to avoiding any queries from them?" For the time being, there was no reason to be concerned; if I kept my gear out of sight and just wandered around, I would be safe.

And so, I moved my gear over to the deck of the "high speed quad ski lift." In the past, that always provided me with a nice quiet place to rest, a level place for cooking, and a wonderful overlook for viewing the land to the northwest. In particular Mount Monadnock, Thoreau's favorite mountain, is most prominent, almost within arms reach just 40 miles distant. On this day unfortunately, she wore a veil of gray mist although, as a tease, from time to time, she dropped her guard and her unmistakable profile appeared, large and daunting.

Boston also wore the shroud of gray mist. A gentle breeze cooled me as I sat in the shade where the temperature was in the low 70° F range.[78] I took a comfortable position watching the sky, the land, the trees and the people as they came and went. When not watching or thinking, I read from my paperback *Walden*. This was relaxing and comfortable until two young employees of the ski area mounted the platform and climbed high into the working mechanism of the lift. After a few minutes, they came down and requested that I move from the platform since they were starting the lift; a wedding party would soon arrive! Well, that was nice—and expensive too, I bet!

So, another move. This time, I returned to the summit and settled down beside the U.S. Army Corps of Engineers radio relay antenna towers. I looked over the grassy plot and thought that it just might be the most level area on the summit—just right for a small tent! A chipmunk appeared from behind a nearby rock nibbling aggressively on a snack that he held in his grasp, one eye on the snack, the other on me. In the bushes down the slope, I noticed four or five sparrows, but not being a birder, I could only speculate. I recorded the following description: black beak, white light gray breast, dark

[78] An official check of the thermometer that is located in the attendant's hut provides a temperature reading of 73.4° F; inside the hut it was 83.5° F.

wings, white and perhaps a touch of red or rust underneath, a slight crest. They preened themselves and darted about the area.

Like any other warm summer day, there were all types of people to be found on the mountain. Howard and I met one elderly gentleman as we were preparing to leave the parking lot for the final climb; an older gentleman, he was huffing and puffing as he labored with an obviously heavy load strapped to his back. He explained that he was loaded with water and magazines and in the process of getting in shape for a trip on the Appalachian Trail. Then, off he went. At about two-thirds of the way up, we passed him again; he was going back down. But this time he was most reticent; it was strictly business as he made his way over the rocks. Strange guy, we commented, but what did we know.

Later, at the summit, before Howard left, we saw him yet again. We waved and he came across the parking lot—not walking a very straight line, I might add. Laughing, I asked him how many times he had been up and down. "Five; I hope to do one more!" Several hours later, I had not seen him return so I imagined that five was the limit.[79]

Another interesting fellow arrived at the summit astride his very distinguished blue racing bike. He was decked out in a United States Postal Service jersey and shorts, identical in appearance to the uniform worn by Lance Armstrong of Tour de France lore. We talked about his 90 mile ride for the day and then he explained to another passerby that the bike was a replica of the Trek™ model made famous by Lance and the USPS ® cycling team. It was #1 of several

---

[79] Actually Howard ran into him one more time when he was going back to the car. I missed seeing him for this his sixth trip of the day!

hundred that were produced and the price tag was in the neighborhood of about $10 grand.

With the deep rumble, so noticeably "Harley", I spied a biker and a female companion as they rolled to a corner of the parking lot; the shiny black bike slowed to a crawl and stopped. They were snared deep into what was obviously a heated argument. Within minutes, having scarcely looked about to enjoy the sights, they donned helmets, cranked the engine and roared down the road headed off the mountain. It was hardly worth the $2.00 admission fee! But then again, they might have solved their problems in the thin air of Wachusett. Priceless!

Noticing a lady pull out a lawn chair and a blanket from the bed of a pick-up, I inquired as to her purpose today. "Are you here for the meteor showers?" I asked. "No, just relaxing." And that was that. I expected to see a number of people here for the beginning of the annual Perseid meteor shower, which would be an attraction in the night sky throughout the coming week.

It was just about 6:00 p.m. when, at last, the wedding party arrived. In full dress, they climbed from the chair lift to the summit and headed to the pond for pictures. A small plane droned overhead, flying quite close to the summit—a mechanical hawk. As I watched, I noticed that the clouds were running from west to east—rather normal here. The plane turned and proceeded to buzz us again. Perhaps he was looking for Thoreau; although, tucked down here by these rocks, I was quite sure that he couldn't find me.

Turning, he pulled away to the south toward the airport at West Boylston; quiet filled the air. An hour later, deep into *Walden*, I stood to look about the lot and saw that there was but one car and two other people on the summit. The ski lift, without warning, had gone silent, the wedding party had left, and a robin struggled against the wind to gain flight. He quietly settled on one of the guy wires supporting the tower. The sun slowly dropped; shadows extended themselves across the parking lot. While the temperature was dropping rather noticeably, I resumed my reading, waiting for sunset, still an hour away at 8:00 pm.[80] After a while, I grew tired of that and decided to walk the Old Indian Trail.

> The blueberries which the mountain afforded, added to the milk we had brought, made our frugal supper, while for entertainment, the even-song of the wood-thrush rung along the ridge. Our eyes rested on no painted ceiling, nor carpeted hall, but on skies of nature's painting, and hills and forests of her embroidery. Before sunset, we rambled along the ridge to the north, while a hawk soared still above us. It was a place where gods might wander, so solemn and solitary, and removed from all contagion with the plain. As the evening came on, the haze was condensed in vapor, and the landscape became more distinctly visible, and numerous sheets of water were brought to light ….[81]

The rocky trail rose just beyond the chairlift drop zone and then, just as quickly, descended to a lush green forest. I found myself in a new world, or perhaps, a new version of the old. The quiet of the ridge was broken by the wondrous voice of the ever-present thrush. Many times have I heard their choir here in the Old Growth Forest.

Thoreau writes that he and Fuller strolled on the ridge just before sunset. With such a small area on the top cap of Wachusett, I was treading on historic ground. The Old Indian Trail runs from the

---

[80] U.S. Naval Observatory, web site, Data Services <http://aa.usno.navy.mil/data/>. The exact time of sunset is 8:00 pm, with twilight ending at 8:31 p.m.

[81] Thoreau, *Excursions* 39.15–27.

summit northwesterly for a quarter of a mile before dropping sharply off the edge of the mountain cap. A few lesser paths venture about, but the well-worn Old Indian Trail, interspersed with outcroppings of rocks and trees and roots, winds gently and peacefully. Meandering slowly along the path, I encountered no others; the last had descended in order to reach the base before darkness. For now, there remained sufficient light to display the deep greens of the Old Growth; clouds gently rolled high in the sky.

Solitary and serene, the promenade is quiet to all but the sounds of nature, a soft summer breeze on my face and the pervasive song of the wood thrush. Nothing has changed over the years.

Seldom have I walked so slowly along this trail. I forced my pace—slower—slower—and slower. It was a newfound peace, quiet to my ears and soft on my feet—a quiet saunter to be sure. The tumult of the summit was gone from my mind, and the trail, the rocks, and the trees no longer familiar as the Old Indian Trail. Monadnock rests beyond my vision and the adjacent hills sit quietly in a blue haze far in the distance. Perhaps I had gone back in time. Would the gods wander here? For sure, they have, they do, and they will.

An old hymn came to mind. Based upon a poem written by Swedish preacher Carl Gustav Boberg in 1885, it was later translated and arranged to the tune of an old Swedish melody.

> *Verse*
> When through the woods and forest glades I wander
> And hear the birds sing sweetly in the trees;
> When I look down from lofty mountain grandeur
> And hear the brook and feel the gentle breeze:
>
> *Refrain*
> Then sings my soul, my Savior God, to Thee:
> How great Thou art, how great Thou art!

Then sings my soul! My Savior God, to Thee,
How great Thou art, how great Thou art![82]

Returning to my pack, the activity level on the summit had mysteriously picked-up. While it was deserted a short while ago, there were now as many as 8 cars and 30 or 40 people. Clearly, this band of visitors was here for the sunset. Several of them were caught gazing skyward: a hawk sighting. It was a scene, like many others, straight from Thoreau's pen: "a hawk soared still above us ...."[83] Two shadows slowly skimmed over the treetops to the west; then four and five and then six. The perpetrators? Red tails, as if dropped like gliders from a nearby airstrip, graced the blue airspace above, in search of small mammals or birds. Gracefully, as if to lull us asleep as we watched, they soared up and down, side to side.

And soon, the floating birds in the sky fell beyond our field of vision. With patience, everyone continued just looking and waiting and waiting ... waiting for the sun's plunge from the sky. It would be the highlight of the evening for some. I raised my finger to the horizon and measured the distance between the sun and the distant horizon. Ten minutes per finger is the rough estimate. I figured sunset would happen in 30 to 40 minutes.

As I waited, I thought of what Will Howarth wrote when I informed him of my plans: "So you are certainly trying something new, recreating the full journey on foot, and that should be very worthwhile and instructive."[84] So ... just what had I learned to this point?

---

[82] Carl Boberg, Hymn, *How Great Thou Art*, Swedish folk melody, "O Store Gud." Verse 2 and refrain. [cited 6/3/08] <http://en.wikipedia.org/wiki/How_ Great_ Thou _Art>.

[83] Thoreau, *Excursions* 39.22.

[84] William Howarth email to author dated 6/29/04.

Well, I'd learned to stay off the macadam; it saves legs. Surely the Indians and all the others doing long distance excursions didn't have to worry about it. Soft ground was the only thing they had to walk on. I learned I could endure; it was a long trip yesterday—28 miles. I've never done quite that much before; I learned many people like to share if you stopped on the side and engaged them. I didn't meet too many, but the ones I did meet were entertaining and enjoyable. I learned that my wife believes in me; God bless her. She stuck with the whole thing; for over a year she has been listening and encouraging ... she understands. And I learned that it is possible to reenact one of Thoreau's walks. There are many things that just haven't changed. Yes, it has been a learning experience, and I haven't even started to put together the written word.

### *8:00 P.M.—Sunset on the Summit*

I returned to the present. I must get back to the sunset; it was just minutes before 8:00 p.m., the official time of sunset.[85] Excitement permeated the scene as everyone gathered on the western rocks at the base of the fire tower. The tiny golden yellow disc slipped into a band of pink haze. The adults seemed to be observing a ritual of silence, speaking to one another in whisper-like voices. Church was in session. Children shrieked and giggled as parents attempted to restrain them and direct their attention to the horizon. The reddish orange orb slipped into a violet band of haze. A dog barked in the background. The children now gazed transfixed by the sight on the horizon; finally, they too became silent. Nothing stirred. I followed

---

[85] U.S. Naval Observatory, web site, Data Services. <http://aa.usno.navy.mil/data/>. On this day in 1842, the sun set at 7.00 p.m. Eastern Standard Time, which would have been 8:00 p.m. had the Eastern Daylight Time system been in place. In that respect, I am getting a real 1842 experience.

the red star, and gradually it became but a pink pinprick in the blue band just above the treetops … extinguished for the day.

For a split second the silence remained. And then a stirring and a shuffling of feet over rocks and gravel could be heard; car doors slammed, a rapid-fire "vroom, vroom" called out in the night. Engines behind me in the parking lot burst to life. The summit was a whir of activity. A single red taillight of a motorcycle disappeared into the dark valley below. More light beams dove into the darkness. It was get-away time; a drive home; kids to bed; and relax for the week ahead. On the summit the patrons have disappeared. Not a bad day at all!

I wandered about the lower level of the summit waiting, waiting—to be sure everyone had left. A green truck appeared, slowed and turned 360°; the driver called to no one in particular but to the stragglers, "It's 8 o'clock and we're locking up. We're locking up." Five minutes later, two sets of taillights wound down the mountain and I was finally alone.

### *8:15 P.M.—Thoreau's Wild—A Night on the Summit*

Just south of the departing sun, Jupiter, the evening star, stood about 15° in elevation, arm-in-arm with the fragile sliver of a moon. As a couple, they would leave the mountain within the hour. The pink sky faded more rapidly now, and then the twinkling of lights from the surrounding towns below the mountain appeared. I could see all; high on the summit, I was invisible to everyone below.

Beside the Army Corps of Engineers Radio Relay Antenna shack, a yellow and black tent, measuring but 6' x 5' x 3', quickly sprang to life. Zzzip—Zzzip went the tent door and I sat safely within—my worldly belongings and me. In no time at all, I was ready for a quiet comfortable night of rest. I noticed that the wind had suddenly risen, gusting perhaps to 20 miles an hour; the tent swayed from side to side, but the stays held fast in the clay. I was good for the night. I remembered Cygnus, high overhead last night at the Buss Tavern; he was missing in action on this night; the clouds came in fast with the wind. Zzzip—up went the sleeping bag zipper. "Good night to all; what a trip."

I slept until about 2:30 a.m. at which time, stronger gusting winds woke me; still the tent stood strong. I looked through the mesh protection and directly overhead, saw a barely visible red beacon slowly turning. I touched the surface of the tent and it was heavy with dampness. Condensation! I fumbled for my shoes and slid them on. Peering outside, the stars were missing; the wind rushed at my face. It was a spirited moment as an angry wind blustered through the trees and over the rocks. I sat and listened. For some moments it was as deafening as a train coming down the tracks; at other times it sheered off to somewhere in the distance for a brief detour. I put on my sneakers. I unzipped the tent door and carefully stepped outside. The wind yanked the flap from my grasp. Flailing at it, I quickly grasped it and secured it behind me.

Carefully I pushed my way against the wind to the rocks just a few feet away. And then, my mind became confused. With the rushing, howling wind, I couldn't hear myself think; the tent was no longer visible; the beacon, as a reference point, was gone; where was I? I had lost my bearings. Disoriented, fear struck me; in the foggy darkness the wind continued whipping and thundering over the rocks. Just that quickly, I was lost at sea! I managed a few steps in the direction from which I came … looking about, nothing seemed to change.

Was this the wild that Thoreau sought and would later discover on Mount Katahdin?[86] Here in the 21st century? I thought Wachusett to be tamed, nature at rest on this crest of a small monadnock. Rarely had I encountered such wind on her slopes. And now a fearsome unexpected force caught me unawares.

Repeated thunderous gusts of wind coming from the north slashed at my face. "Don't panic, move slowly," I told myself. I struggled to control my mind and my actions. Looking up again, a faint red glow appeared. Moving slowly and carefully in that direction a triangular silhouette materialized—at last, the door of the tent. I dove for cover and comfort. First the tent flap and then the sleeping bag. Zzzip Zzzip. From inside, I looked straight up through the mesh of my tent, but the rotating red light was invisible once again. The murky haze had swallowed me completely, swallowed my tent, and swallowed the whole mountain, I was sure. And unexpectedly, I had found it; this was Thoreau's "wild."

Light filtered through the tent screen and stirred my consciousness. I rolled over and cracked an eye, only one to be sure, to peer at my watch—5:04 a.m. I turned on my back and the beacon was only barely visible. Heavy morning fog continued to roll over the mountaintop. The whereabouts of the lookout station, 30 yards away when last seen, was a mystery to me. Had it come crashing down in the night? Probably not, but in the thick rolling fog, I could not locate it. Was my mind not functioning? Where lie my senses?

I turned away from the light tower, dozing on and off, thinking of home and the family. Normally, I would be up with our dog,

---

[86] Thoreau relates a frighteningly similar experience in *The Maine Woods*. Princeton: Princeton University Press, 1972. 62.32–65.9. While the book describes his three trips to the interior, it is in the narrative entitled "Ktaadn," that he describes his startling climb up the mountain.

Chuck, and getting ready for work at this hour. But today, my sole job was to return home in time and distance from the western retreat.

At 6:25 a.m., the fog bank remained as it continued to roll across the summit slopes. A yellow disc appeared, on occasion, in the east, but visibility beyond the gunnels of the ship remained low at best. With a steaming cup of coffee, I wandered to the ski shack, just below the tent. There, I checked the thermometer and found the outside air temperature to be 63° F; inside the shack it was 69.6° F. With just about the same cubic area, that's my guess as to the temperature in the tent. Reclining in one of the chairs, I comfortably looked over the scene, breathed deeply of the cool morning air and felt very much alive.

> All memorable events, I should say, transpire in morning time and in a morning atmosphere. The Vedas say, "All intelligences awake with the morning." Poetry and art, and the fairest and the most memorable of the actions of men date from such an hour. All poets and heroes, like Memnon, are the children of Aurora, and emit their music at sunrise. … Morning is when I am awake and there is a dawn in me.[87]

But this scene was not unique. You could find it on just about any mountaintop in the Eastern United States. I remembered a hike to the summit of Mount Washington several years back in time; then as now, I was mired in a thick impenetrable ocean of gray. Visibility was almost non-existent. Here on Wachusett, I have seen this many times in the past.

> At the top, I was greeted by a total encapsulation of the summit by a gently rolling fog. Standing in

[87] Thoreau, *Walden.* 89.28–90.3.

> the center of the parking lot, atop the compass rose stand, I could barely recognize the outline of the landscape before it plunged off to the unknown. I felt as if I was standing on the cap of a mushroom and beyond its edge, all around, was a damp, misty unknown. I wandered to the edge of the cap, as is my usual practice, and I lost all sense of orientation.[88]

Overhead, blue sky slowly penetrated the damp gray blanket. I expected the clouds to soon run away and that a fine summer experience would be the order of the day.

"Woof, woof, woof" A distinct and familiar sound was heard over the horizon to the south. "Those aren't wild dogs," I thought. "We'll have visitors in a few minutes." And sure enough, within minutes, two ghoulish faceless human shapes appeared on the horizon of the summit, walking slowly, rising over the lip of the parking area. They began to circumnavigate the graveled summit area, slowly moving in a large circle. Reaching the paved road from which they began, they turned in my direction, waved, and disappeared into the fog, down the road, and out of sight, apparently with their dogs in tow. I watched for several seconds trying to keep them in focus, but a gentle gust of wind from the north erased their outlines as quickly as they had appeared. Were they real people or perhaps ghosts from the past? In search of Lucy Keyes? Thoreau and Fuller? Hummm??

A break in the mist, the sun broke through for a moment, and I was reminded of my breakfast now hot on the stove. A steamy mist came from the lid of the pot; to the oatmeal, I added a large handful of fresh blueberries—just perfect on an empty stomach! I returned to my senses, reasoning that the visitors probably arrived in hopes of

---

[88] Robert Young, *Wachusett Chronologically–I,* Journal entry dated 10/14/2001.

seeing a grand sunrise and quickly realizing that it was not to be on this morning, turned, and headed homeward to the clear skies below. I was alone again. Breakfast was soon over and it was time to move on.

I began the task of turning down the tent and repacking. The breeze continued to push the thinning clouds. And while I couldn't see them, members of the ever-present thrush family had just warbled the opening stanza of the day.

### *9:00 A.M. August 8—Departure from the Summit*

The roar of a passing truck was heard just below the trail as I approached Mountain Road. It was almost 9:00 a.m. and the morning had just begun to heat up. Reaching the boundary of the Reservation and the trailhead parking lot, I dropped my pack since I had agreed to a meeting with Emily Young, a reporter for the Sentinel & Enterprise newspaper. Howard, if he could make it, was also scheduled meet me at the trailhead.

The parking lot was empty when I arrived. The sun had not risen to the appointed ninth hour, but still, I needed to pass the time. It was a day for walking rather than waiting. I couldn't leave until I had given Emily and Howard ample time to arrive. With that thought, I just wandered about the adjacent meadow amateurishly checking the residents. I found a number of treasures.

> There are butterflies down here, goldenrod, grass, flowers, Queen Anne's lace, some red clover, white clover, some wild strawberries, a bird feather—can't really tell what it is, some other kind of flower, some kind of herb, looks like, Dutchman's … no, looks like some kind of pea pod thing, purple flowers, just wandering around, bright yellow star shaped flowers, … probably some poison ivy too. God knows it will be miracle if I don't catch

> some on my legs with the gutters and tight areas I've been walking in these past three days. Red clover as well and 1…2…3…4…5 maple saplings right in the middle. I tell you … this has to be … I'll read it over again. Has to be his maple stand … Hear a car coming; maybe that's Howard.[89]

In time Emily and Howard arrived; the interview was conducted; the car was packed; and again, I was on my way. It was just a few minutes after 10:00 a.m. The home hearth beckoned.

### *10:00 A.M.—East Princeton*

Actually, the route home was a "straight shot" off the mountain, up and over the Monoosnock Ridge and down into South Leominster. From the parking lot at Gregory Road there were a couple of decent hills yet to climb, but my mind told me: "it's all downhill from here."[90] And from that thought, I had a light spring in my step; warm sunshine beamed down on me; everything's coming up roses; my heart sang out in happiness.

Gregory Road never fails to remind me of a time long past. The steep descent, along with the narrow, winding, almost single lane dirt road, is befitting of a Thoreau era journey. Halfway down the hill, I raised my head to look beyond the stone wall; I searched for the family of wild turkeys. I saw nothing so perhaps it was too hot for them to stray from cover.

A chain saw irritatingly buzzed away close at hand. It cut the quiet and peacefulness of the forest as deftly as the wood. "Waaa,

---

[89] Young, Transcript of notes recorded throughout the journey, 2005.

[90] The profile of the hike from the summit to our back door was definitely downhill, exactly as I suspected. The elevation change is approximately 1,600 feet. There are some rolling hills, but it is decidedly downhill! Software: National Geographic – Northeastern, USA, maps powered by TOPO! computer software, San Francisco: National Geographic, 2002.

Waaa"—the modern version of the two-man cross cut does quick work of the tree. Between cuts, I heard birds screeching—crying out angrily at the desecration of their home?

On Beamon Road, a Waste Management™ recycling truck sped toward us, passed, and disappeared around the bend. It's a public attempt at cutting back on our waste of natural resources. Since its entry into the mainstream of public consciousness in the mid-1980s, it has been a successful endeavor although we have a ways to go.

The road twists to the right and down a grade as we approached the intersection of Beamon Road with Hobbs Road. A green island, bedecked with yellow and blue flowers sits at the intersection. It is there, to be sure, with some amount of angst and sadness that I took leave of my brothers, Fuller and Thoreau. We wished each other well and promised to correspond; we shook hands and parted—for the time. Continuing onward toward Sterling, Lancaster and Harvard, they rested for the night in Harvard before continuing their journey the next day. Fuller continued to Groton, while good weather led Thoreau to his beloved Concord.

And so, I took a less traveled road, Hobbs Road, and headed onward—to the highway below, to Leominster and the yellow house we call home.

It was 10:47 a.m. and a parade of cars was passing down Route 140. But a busy parade of cars allows no open space for a pedestrian to cross from one side to the other. They zoomed wildly past me, one after the other, and then came the whine of a motorcycle. Waaaaa. Finally, separation … I sprinted for safety of the other side. Here, Hobbs Road continues for a short distance within the boundary of Princeton before it passes to Leominster. Before we arrived at the boundary, we took a break for something to eat and drink. It was warm, warmer than yesterday, but I only had ten miles to go today.

Refreshed, I marched over the hill, sauntering my way homeward. Physically, the roadway is not difficult, but in spirit, I realized that I already missed my brothers. The sun beat down in search of me—another attempt to thwart my physical efforts and to melt my cheerful mind. But this battle had already been won. Nothing could stop me, and I soon found myself atop the Monoosnock Ridge overlooking a land that became more familiar with each downhill step. Rounding a final turn, I had yet another big yellow house in view. There, hanging at the side door, awaiting the saunterer's arrival, I found a welcome-home note from my biggest supporter, my wife, Kathleen. Months ago she said, "You should walk it." Months later, she said, "You walked it … congratulations."

> To travel and "descry new lands" is to think new thoughts and have new imaginings. In the spaces of thought are the reaches of land and water over which men go and come. The landscape lies fair within. The deepest and most original thinker is the farthest travelled.[91]

## *After the Journey*

Days, weeks and months have passed, and I have walked the trails of Wachusett many times since Howard and I joined Henry and Richard on that weekend in August. Each visit represents another adventure, another learning experience, and another memory. But now, Wachusett has taken on a new dimension. Indeed, I knew the

---

[91] Thoreau, *Journal 1: 1837–1844*, 171.10–15. Entry dated "Aug. 13th 1840." Thoreau found the phrase "to descry new lands" from either readings of Milton in *Paradise Lost, Book I* or from a reading of William Hazlitt's *Why Distant Objects Please*, which may be found in *Table Talk: Essays on Men and Manners* (1822). For "A Walk to Wachusett," see *Excursions* 31.25–29.

mountain before the weekend of August 6, 2005, but it was a shallow understanding, narrow in scope. Wachusett was simply a land mass represented within the boundaries of the reservation map.

Now, when the profile of the glorious monadnock appears before me, I see her as well as the long hot road we traveled to reach her summit. July 19, 1842 comes alive. My mind passes by the roadside litter, the busy gas stations and farm stands, the industrial buildings, the macadam roads, the fields, the woodlots; so much has changed; it matters not. Beneath today's reality lies yesterday's reality.

And suddenly I cough dusty clouds drawn from the road by hot summer winds; my thirst is quenched by the cool streams; I enjoy conversation with the native farmers; song comes as sweetly from open schoolhouse windows as from the tree tops; gusty winds send chills through my body on the summit; stars dance overhead; I taste the berries and smell the medicinal aroma of the herbs that grow along the roadside; silence spreads over the land as peace flows from the ocean up the Merrimack River to the Concord, the Sudbury, the Assabet, the Nashua, to Monadnock and other mountains to the far north, to Greylock in the west. It all rushes back; my heart races and I feel aglow.

My brother, Thoreau, experienced Nature; he lived for Nature.

> In the street and in society I am almost invariably cheap and dissipated, my life is unspeakably mean. … But alone in distant woods or fields, in unpretending sprout-lands or pastures tracked by rabbits, even in a bleak and, to most, cheerless day, like this, when a villager would be thinking of his inn, I come to myself, I once more feel myself grandly related, and that cold and solitude are friends of mine. I suppose that this value, in my case, is equivalent to what others get by churchgoing and prayer. I come home to my solitary woodland walk as the homesick go home. I thus dispose of the su-

> perfluous and see things as they are, grand and beautiful. I have told many that I walk every day about half the daylight, but I think they do not believe it. I wish to get the Concord, the Massachusetts, the America, out of my head and be sane a part of every day.[92]

I love my time in church, but many a Sunday visit for services has been passed in lieu of a walk in the woods. There too, I meet my Maker and the beauty that He has given us if we take the time to take it in.

I found the route; I re-enacted the journey; I discovered that life in the 1840's still exists; I learned the truth about Thoreau's Wild; I came away with another view of this great land that has been alive and well for so long. And like Thoreau, I had but to travel only a few miles to find it.

---

[92] Thoreau. *The Journal of Henry David Thoreau in Fourteen Volumes Bound as Two.* ed. Bradford Torrey and Francis H. Allen. (New York: Dover, 1962) 1104. Entry dated January 7, 1857.

# July 1842: Thoreau's Journey

> Truly men do not have to travel to seek knowledge—for if they stay at home—she will travel to find them.
>
> —*Journal Volume 1* (437.2-4)

### *The Beginning*

Meteorologically the statistics for Tuesday July 19, 1842 are as follows: civil twilight began at 3:50 a.m.; the sun rose at 4:24 a.m.; sunset was at 7:18 pm; and twilight ended at 7:51 pm.[93,94] The moon was extremely bright during the night as ninety-three percent (93%) of its disk was illuminated. It would be a full moon before Thoreau and Fuller returned two days hence. According to the Meteorological Record,[95] the weather was "Hot with thunder." This would, of course, be very much a typical summer day in the 1800's, the 1900's, and even the 2000's. At the time of the journey, Thoreau was 25 years old; Fuller was 18.

And thus, with knapsacks containing a tent for shelter, books by Virgil and Wordsworth, matches, and various unidentified items,[96] the two began their journey on foot to the monadnock called Wachusett seated on the western horizon. From the very first step taken that morning and until they reached the summit the following day, written details about the roads traveled are sketchy at best, no matter whose account is read. Aside from identifying towns through which they

---

[93] Daylight Saving Time was introduced to the United States in 1916 during World War I. Accordingly, all times in 1842 are stated in Eastern Standard Time.

[94] U.S. Naval Observatory, web site, Data Services [Cited 2005]< http://aa.usno.navy.mil/data/>.

[95] Leonard Hill, *Hill Meteorological and Chronological Register* (Moses Bates, 1869) 221.

[96] A detailed list of what might have been in the knapsack is gleaned from notes of his 1860 journey to Monadnock. See Thoreau, *Thoreau in the Mountains*, Commentary by W. Howarth. 358.

passed and naming some of the rivers or streams they encountered, the exact route is unspecified.[97]

But, a close reading of the essays does provide some subtle, and some not so subtle clues, as to their whereabouts throughout the trip. And from that information, it is quite possible to establish a reasonably accurate route for the complete journey. We know they left from Emerson's house; Fuller tells us that. And from both, we know the outbound portion of the trip concluded on the summit of Mt. Wachusett. What course lay between these points? And how did they return? That was my challenge.

In 1842 Thoreau was living at the home of friend and mentor Ralph Waldo Emerson. There, he worked as a laborer for the Emerson family, helping about the house and the grounds.[98] When retired from his daily chores, he had ample time to write, to saunter, and to read. One might theorize that they left from *Bush*, but indeed Thoreau wrote nothing of their specific starting point of the walk.

It is left to his traveling companion, Richard Fuller, a student at Harvard and a disciple of Emerson, to elaborate upon the departure in his account of the trip titled, "Visit to the Wachusett."[99] From his essay we learn details of the departure and other background information.

His trip actually began the day prior, Monday July 18, 1842, when he left Cambridge and walked over the hills of Lexington and West Cambridge to Emerson's home in Concord, a distance of approxi-

[97] Neither Thoreau nor Fuller provided a detailed accounting of the route.

[98] Walter Harding, *The Days of Henry Thoreau: A Biography*, (New York: Dover Publications, 1982) 126.

[99] Fuller, 1–4.

mately 18 miles. He reflects on that portion of the journey in great detail, specifying in rather flowery language his reasons for the trip.

The semester at Harvard had come to a close, and apparently he was tired from the work of study and learning. "I resolved to go in search of Pan, since he could not come to me," he writes. Later he amplifies this thought: "other adventures than Nature offered we avoided; and we listen[ed], as we went along, to her harmony, thinking that perchance some note of novel sweetness might be struck, which should charm our heart, and awaken within us some new sentiment."[100]

And so, on Monday afternoon, the 18th of July, he arrived at *Bush* and was welcomed by both Emerson and Thoreau. The fact that he arrived in Concord on one day and left for Wachusett early the following morning would appear to be a clear indication that the trip was planned in advance.

While this journey occurs early in Thoreau's career, it is most likely that he did a certain amount of advance planning prior to departure, perhaps not to ascertain the route but to gain familiarity with the countryside and what they might encounter along the way. Resources that might have been utilized include John Hayward's *The New England Gazetteer*, Charles Theodore Russell's *History of Princeton*, and Peter Whitney's *History of Worcester County*. Another useful resource might have been town maps that resulted from a directive of the Commonwealth in 1830.

Without delay, one understands that Thoreau had often gazed over the horizon to view the mountains in the west. In those days, it was quite possible to see distant features from the tops of moderately

---

[100] Fuller, 1–4.

sized hills. The forests had been cut back for two reasons: clear land was needed for pastures, and equally as important, felled trees provided the primary source of heat during the cold New England winters. Approximately 70 percent of the land had been cleared by mid-century.[101] On October 12, 1840, a journal entry is made: "… but now that I am left alone, I see the blue peaks in the horizon, and am homesick."[102] On August 4, 1841, while standing on Nawshawtuct, he writes, "— Here, in sight of Wachusett and these rivers and woods, my mind goes singing to itself of other themes than taxation."[103]

Thus he begins: "Summer and winter our eyes had rested on the dim outline of the mountains in our horizon …."[104] And while "standing on the Concord cliffs,"[105] Thoreau—once again—ponders the possibilities of a trip westward to Wachusett.

Following a flowery poetic introduction with a poem written but rejected for publication by Margaret Fuller, editor of the literary magazine *The Dial* and older sister of Richard, he continues, "At a cool and early hour …."[106] A habitual early riser, he loved the experience of the morning and what it served him. But it is Fuller who clears the air concerning the time of departure; he is very specific: "The morning of the next day arrived, Mr. Thoreau and myself … at

---

[101] Robert D. Richardson Jr., *Henry Thoreau, A Life of the Mind* (Los Angeles University of California Press, 1986) 16.

[102] Thoreau, *Journal Volume 1 188.20–21.* Entry dated "Oct 12th 1840."

[103] Thoreau, *Journal Volume 1 315.23–25.* Dateline: "Nawshawtuct. Wednesday Aug. 4th 1841."

[104] Thoreau, *Excursions* 29.5–6.

[105] Thoreau, *Excursions* 29.13–14.

[106] Thoreau, *Excursions* 31.30.

about quarter of five, started."[107] There! We have it; the starting time is defined as well as the names of the participants. It is interesting to note that throughout his entire account, Thoreau never mentions Fuller by name.

## *Concord to Acton and Stow*

From the "Concord cliffs," Thoreau jumps ahead, beyond the Concord border, to Acton. He advises, "my companion and I passed rapidly through Acton and Stow …."[108] Fuller, too, skips their passage from Concord with nary a word. Other than his clear declaration that the journey began at Emerson's home, his first mention of any location along the route is well into his essay: "we had got onward, and soon came to a wood that lies between Concord and Stowe."[109] On the surface, it appears that both men were anxious to escape the clutches of home. For Thoreau at least, it was a sign that, in Concord, Acton and Stow, he was well within his comfort zone. His physical map had not yet been challenged; that would come later in Bolton, when they stopped at Great Brook, and we learn that he was unable to identify the stream beside which they rested.

In 1842, should one have wished to head in a westerly direction from Concord Center along a convenient path that terminated at Mount Wachusett, one question asked might have been, "what roads are available?" Being well versed in the geographies of towns in Massachusetts, Thoreau probably had a number of possibilities in mind:

---

[107] Eastern Standard Time. Today that time would advance one hour to 5:45 a.m. Daylight Saving Time. On the 19th, sunrise was at 4:24 a.m. and the sun, if not behind cloud cover as indicated in the weather forecast, would have been visible just over the horizon.

[108] Thoreau, *Excursions* 31.31–32.

[109] Fuller, 3.

Sudbury Road, Marlborough Road, the Great Road, Lancaster Road, and Stow Road.[110] Of these, the primary east-west route was unquestionably The Great Road. But first, they would have to reach it.

One of the earliest (circa.1630) routes in the area was called the Bay Path; it ran from Cambridge to Springfield, passing through the towns of Wayland, Sudbury, Stow, Lancaster, Princeton, Brookfield, Warren, Brimfield, and Springfield (and later south to Hartford, and west into New York State).[111] This was clearly the route of the Reverend Thomas Prince as he made his way from Cambridge to Princeton in the early 1700s. In the 1800's the Great Road, following portions of the Bay Path from Cambridge to Bolton, was one of the primary east-west routes in the area. At the time, it was a major artery linking civilized regions of the east with the unknown and the somewhat barbaric wilderness beyond the western horizon. Stagecoaches traveled the route, carrying passengers between the eastern communities and those to the west in Massachusetts, New Hampshire, Vermont and New York. Rest stops and horse exchanges were scheduled along the route. Indeed, the Great Road provided a most favorable option for travel toward the mountain called Wachusett.

From Concord, there were only three logical ways to reach this vibrant artery: the Sudbury Road, the Marlborough Road and the Lancaster Road. But, the first two options led directly to Sudbury and following assumption 2, they would not have ventured along either of these routes. Furthermore, had they taken either of these

---

110 On his survey of this area in 1852, he called it "Old Road to Stow"; today it is called "Old Stow Road." A map of Acton by Horace Tuttle in 1890 (MDCCCXC) calls this "Stow Road (before 1735)." Acton was incorporated in 1735.

111 George F. Marlowe, *The Old Bay Paths: Their Villages and Byways and their Stories* (New York: Hastings House. 1942) 14.

routes, Acton would have been bypassed completely and that town is specifically noted in each rendition of the trip. Only the final choice remained—Lancaster Road.

Fronting Emerson's house is the Cambridge Road, over which Fuller traveled on the 18th of July to arrive at *Bush*.[112] And but a few rods toward the village, the Cambridge Road joins one of the earliest major thoroughfares in the town of Concord, the Lexington Road. In 1636 it was the first road in Concord designated for public use.[113,114] Originally it was called the Bay Road, later the Boston Road, and finally the Lexington Road. And so, early the following morning Thoreau and Fuller walked this road a short distance to the town green whereupon they headed west along Main Street, known in times past as the Lancaster Road and also as the Stow Road.[115] As early as the 1650's, it had followed footpaths as a means of reaching Lancaster, the next settlement to the west.

The Lancaster Road led directly to the mills situated on the western bounds of Concord. It crossed the Assabet to the north side of the river at Derby's Bridge and continued to the mill section of town, Westvale or Damon's Mills. From there, Acton was within easy reach

---

112 Fuller, 3.

113 Ann McCarthy Forbes, prepared for the *Town of Bolton, 1998 Historical Properties Survey.* <http://www.townofbolton.com/Pages/BoltonMA_TownHistory/toc> Transportation Routes (1776–1830). Roads from Lancaster to Boston are often referred to or designated as the old Lancaster Road, "Boston Road", the Great Road and, more recently, Main Street or Route 117.

114 Charles Hosmer Walcott, *Concord Roads, notes by* , 1. The Concord Free Public Library, Special Collections. Charles H. Walcott Papers Series II: Foldered Materials, Folder II, 2.10.

115 Over time, the names of some roads changed. Some parts of them might face a name change while other parts remained the same. Conventional names might have been used on a given map, but the same region produced in a different era or by a different cartographer might use other names. Roads that crossed boundary lines between districts are particularly problematic.

just a short distance up the road. With no bridge across the Assabet at that point in time, the road, often called the Road to Stow,[116] turned north of the river to high ground and followed a wide sweeping arc into Acton[117] whence it ran parallel to the Assabet in a south westerly direction. Crossing the town line into Stow,[118] it continued a short distance before joining The Great Road in the community of Stow Commons.[119]

In a personal summarization of the history of Concord roads, Charles H. Walcott, wrote of the Lancaster or Stow Road:

> Then, in order to avoid the river, it [Lancaster Road] turned to the high ground on the right as it now runs over the railroad and through miles of woodland passing the boundary line of Concord Village (Acton) and bearing towards the southwest as well as the course of the river and the character of the ground would permit through Fletcher Corner and to the northward of where the powder mills and Mills of the Assabet Manufacturing Co. now are, making a great sweep in the westerly part of Maynard and running through Stow and Bolton on the present main road through these towns.[120]

---

[116] Before the incorporation of the town of Acton in 1735, her landholdings were owned by Concord. Thus, we have the origin of the road's namesake, *The Road to Stow*. Stow, on the other hand, was incorporated in 1683 from land, at the time, also owned by Concord. This explains why we have references also to the Lancaster Road.

[117] Acton was incorporated in 1735 from lands owned by Concord, specifically, the land for Acton was the former Concord Village. Since Stow, before 1735, lay adjacent to Concord, the pathway leading to Stow was called The Stow Road.

[118] Today, this border crossing would be into the town of Maynard, incorporated in 1871 from lands in northern Sudbury (Assabet Village) and eastern Stow.

[119] Now called Lower Village Common.

[120] Charles Hosmer Walcott, *Concord Roads, notes by* , 1. The Concord Free Public Library, Special Collections. Charles H. Walcott Papers Series II: Foldered Materials, Folder II, 2.10.

Today, the section of road that ran from the north side of the river at Damon's Mills to Independence Road in Acton is a lost piece of the town infrastructure. Close examination of a survey of the Damon's Mills complex, dated September 15, 1851,[121] drafted by Thoreau himself, provides evidence of its one time existence. Between dotted lines, he wrote, "Old Road to Stow." This passageway is parallel to and north of the bed of The Fitchburg Railroad, which cut through the countryside from Concord to Acton. No further detail or explanation is available on his survey document, but early maps of Acton[122] indicate that, just after crossing the town line, the roadbed turned south through a dense wooded area to eventually intersect the Road to Carlisle (north-bound from Sudbury). From the intersection, it continued south to Fletcher Corner west of the Powder Mills before making a westerly turn over Pompasitticut Hill and on to the Great Road. This would easily traverse the path cited by Walcott. The bulk of the north-south passageway has been known as Concord Road but is now designated as Parker Street. It runs from School Street in a southerly direction to Maynard,[123] where it is known as Concord Road.

Connecting roads from one town map to another—especially if the maps being reviewed were drafted by different surveyors or were drafted in different periods of time—can be difficult and confusing.

---

121 Thoreau, Land and Property Surveys. The Concord Free Public Library, Henry David Thoreau Land & Property Surveys, *Acton/Concord Town Line … [Sept 15,1851]* [cited 2005]. < http://www.concordlibrary.org/scollect/Thoreau_surveys/1.htm>.

122 John G. Hales, *Plan of the Town of Acton* 1830.

123 The town of Maynard was incorporated in 1871 from land grants provided by both Sudbury (a small village called Assabet Village) and Stow. In 1842, this section of Maynard was owned by Stow and this road passed into the eastern section of Stow—thus the name East Stow Road.

Surveyor Jabez Brown, in November 1794, completed a plan for the Town of Acton in which he shows a road segment that ran southwesterly from a point south of Lawsbrook Road to the Acton-Stow border about a quarter mile west of the Assabet River. On his survey, this road is called East Stow Road; it is most likely the same as the "Old Stow Road" indicated on later Acton maps as well as on Thoreau's survey. On the 1830 map of Concord, this road is unlabeled; it simply heads toward and across the Acton-Concord town line. The 1830 map of Acton very neatly meets the lines of the 1830 Concord map, as one might expect, since surveyor John G. Hales completed both.

Today, a short segment of existing road at Damon's Mills still carries the name "Old Stow Road." With the construction of the bridge over the Assabet at Westvale in 1843, and the extension of Lancaster Road south to the Powder Mills of Sudbury on the eastern banks of the Assabet, improved access to the Great Road was provided. From that point in time, Stow Road became the "Old Stow Road"—old and of little use. This section of roadway (north of the river to Independence Road/Parker Street) would soon be discontinued as a public roadway; official discontinuance came much later in 1930.[124] The right-of-way for this "connector" was taken over by the construction of The Fitchburg Railroad in 1844.[125,126] What exists to-

---

124 Walcott, *Concord Roads, notes by.* Folder I.

125 Running northward from the western shore line of Walden Pond, the railroad bed cut a path to the Depot at which point it turned sharply to the west, whence it followed a course somewhat parallel to Main Street (Lancaster Road/Stow Road) crossing the Assabet north of Derby's Bridge. Continuing in this direction, it ran just north of Damon's Mills, crossed the boundary separating Concord and Acton, and forged ahead to South Acton and points west.

126 Ann McCarthy Forbes, *West Concord: Survey of Historical and Architectural Resources* (Concord: Concord Historical Commission, 1989) 10.

day is a small segment of roadway off Main Street (Route 62) called "Old Stow Road." After a distance of about a half-mile, it becomes Hillside Avenue as it continues another half mile before intersecting with Lawsbrook Road.

And so Thoreau and Fuller headed southwest along the Lancaster/Stow Road. The road skips through Acton—the actual mileage being only 3 or 4 miles before passing the granite marker indicating passage into Stow.

### *Stow*

As a native of Concord, Thoreau was surely familiar with route to Stow; Fuller was also comfortable with the environs. He attended Stow Academy only 8 years prior to the walk, that being 1834. At the time, he was a lad of 10 years of age while his brother Eugene, nine years his senior,[127] "kept the academy." His parents often visited from their new home in Groton. "I used to ride with them as far as they would let me walk back; and then watch the departing chaise wistfully, as my father and mother turned back and smiled."[128]

Thoreau's essay provides one additional clue that favorably marks his position along this route: "… stopping to rest and refresh us on the bank of a small stream, a tributary of the Assabet, in the latter town [Stow]."[129]

The stream to which he refers is Pratt's Brook, a small stream that crossed the highway in what was then the northeast corner of Stow. In 1871 that section of Stow was relinquished, along with land

---

127 Margaret Fuller Chronology, [Cited 2006]. <http://courses.washington.edu/hum523/fuller/Chronology.shtml>

128 Richard Fuller, 4.

129 Thoreau, *Excursions* 31.32–34.

east of the river owned by Sudbury, to the newly incorporated town of Maynard.

Upon reaching Summer Street, the Lancaster Road passed to the north and west of the mills, intersecting the Great Road in the vicinity of Pompasitticut or Pomcitticut Hill.[130]

And so, by mid-morning the two found themselves in Stow Lower Common following the sun west on the Great Road. Along the road, especially in a town such as Stow, heavy traffic flowed in both directions … all types of carriages, stagecoaches, teams of oxen, wagons of hay and produce as well as local business folk. The road today is, with minor diversions and changes in its course, the same as it was many years ago. Different names were used at along the way, but essentially it was the Great Road, the Bay Path, the Lancaster Road, or today, Route 117.

Along the Great Road, Thoreau and Fuller passed a vast countryside of farmlands and orchards as they made their way toward Bolton, the adjacent town to the west.[131]

> This part of our route lay through the country of hops, which plant perhaps supplies the want of the vine in American scenery, and may remind the traveller of Italy, and the South of France, whether he traverses the country when the hop-fields, as then, present solid and regular masses of verdure, hanging in graceful festoons from pole to pole, the cool coverts where lurk the gales which refresh the way-farer, or in September, when the women and children, and the neighbors from far and near, are gathered to pick the hops into long troughs, or later still, when the poles stand piled in vast pyra-

---

[130] Beer's *Atlas of Middlesex County*–1875. Also map of the Town of Acton–1830

[131] Peter Whitney, *The History of The County of Worcester, in the Commonwealth of Massachusetts* (Worcester: Thomas, 1793) 177. Bolton was incorporated in 1738 from land owned by Lancaster.

mids in the yards, or lie in heaps by the roadside.[132]

They crossed a number of streams, some of them several times. Specifically, Great Brook was recorded as a waypoint along the route; it crosses the Great Road twice in the eastern part of Bolton. This region marks the western edge of the Assabet watershed. It is also at this point that one suspects that Thoreau has reached the outer limits of his physical map. No longer does he feel himself to be knowledgeable in the ways of this land.

> The mower in the adjacent meadow could not tell us the name of the brook on whose banks we had rested, or whether it had any, but his younger companion, perhaps his brother, knew that it was Great Brook.[133]

### *Bolton*

Making their way into the center of Bolton by late morning, the first thought was probably that it would soon be a good time to rest and refresh. With a natural affinity to mountains and hills, the choice was obvious—the hillside of Watoquadoc, and with a well-chosen route, they could pass almost directly over the top. There were two ways they might have traveled beyond Bolton Center toward South Lancaster. Both routes[134] were open for travel in 1842, and both would have provided them with a view of Wachusett to the west and its sister mountains to the north.

One option was to continue along the Great Road approximately

---

132 Thoreau, *Excursions* 33.10–22.

133 Thoreau, *Excursions* 32.28–32.

134 The History of Bolton, Massachusetts. <http://www.townofbolton.com/Pages/BoltonMA_TownHistory/toc>. "The history provided here is taken from the 1998 Historical Properties Survey prepared for the Bolton Historical Commission by Anne McCarthy Forbes, Preservation Consultant. That work was, in turn, based on an earlier inventory of properties prepared by Esther K. Whitcomb."

one mile beyond the Center to Wilder Road. This was actually the course of the North Branch of the Bay Path, which led to the southwest and the boundary with Lancaster. This lower road reaches an elevation of about 500 feet while the summit of Watoquadoc rests just above at an elevation of 618 feet. A view of the valley is clear from this elevation although not as open as from the top of the hill.

> Before noon we had reached the highlands overlooking the valley of Lancaster, (affording the first fair and open prospect into the west,) and there, on the top of a hill, in the shade of some oaks, near to where a spring bubbled out from a leaden pipe, we rested during the heat of the day, reading Virgil, and enjoying the scenery. It was such a place as one feels to be on the outside of the earth, for from it we could, in some measure, see the form and structure of the globe. There lay Wachusett, the object of our journey, lowring upon us with unchanged proportions, though with a less ethereal aspect than had greeted our morning gaze, while further north, in successive order, slumbered its sister mountains along the horizon.[135]

But it was the second option that would take them more directly to the top of the great hill before them. A turn to the southwest at Watoquadoc Hill Road runs to the South Branch of the Bay Path and thence to the top of the hill where a wide sweeping view to the north and west is spectacular. Either path will suffice, and eventually, they found their way to the top of Watoquadoc, a key landmark on the trip.

Indeed, from the hillside of Watoquadoc, one can view Wachusett as well as the sister mountains Grand Monadnock, Watatic, and those of the Wapack Range. Resting on the hillside, Thoreau

---

[135] Thoreau, *Excursions* 33.19–33.

begs us to pay attention to the land about us. Clearly, he was aware of the fact that they were resting at a point of demarcation between the Assabet watershed and that of the Nashua.

> The lay of the land hereabouts is well worthy the attention of the traveller. The hill on which we were resting makes part of an extensive range, running from south-west to north-east, across the country, and separating the waters of the Nashua from those of the Concord, whose banks we had left in the morning, and by bearing in mind this fact, we could easily determine whither each brook was bound that crossed our path. Parallel to this, and fifteen miles further west, beyond the deep and broad valley in which lie Groton, Shirley, Lancaster, and Boylston, runs the Wachusett range, in the same general direction.[136] The descent into the valley on the Nashua side, is by far, the most sudden; and a couple of miles brought us to the southern branch of the Nashua, a shallow but rapid stream, flowing between high and gravelly banks.[137]

A short distance over the crest of the hill in a westerly direction, Wilder Road joins Old Bay Road and the path rolls and winds deeper and deeper into the valley of the Nashuay.

## *Lancaster*

Old Bay Road soon reaches Lancaster just east of the South Branch of the Nashua River at a small section of town called Old Commons or Lancaster Commons. In the early to mid-1800s, this road was heavily trafficked as the Post Road to Boston through Bolton, Stow and Concord. Maps of Lancaster dated 1879 call this the

---

[136] It is 13.7 miles to be exact, 285° TN.

[137] Thoreau, *Excursions* 34.25–35.4.

"Mail Road from Petersham and Greenfield to Boston."[138] Beyond Old Commons, the road descends farther to the Intervale Lots, crossing the river at Atherton Bridge. Upstream a short distance, the North Branch meets the South Branch and flows northward seeking the Concord and eventually the Merrimack River.

Crossing the river and the intervale, the track continues to South Lancaster. There, it crosses Main Street (Route 70), runs south of George Hill, and takes dead aim at Sterling as the "Post Road to Sterling." Today, it is called Sterling Road or more formally Route 62.

The decision on what approach to take into Sterling is actually made in Lancaster. Instead of taking the Post Road to Sterling, one could continue on the Post Road to Worcester for another ½ mile and then take Redstone Hill Road north at the intersection. This leads directly over Redstone Hill, whence it drops immediately into Sterling.

This ½ mile stretch of the Post Road to Worcester is now called Deershorn Road; when I reached that point, I remember commenting to Howard that although it was possible to take it and head over Redstone Hill, it just didn't feel right.[139] It actually felt like it was out of the way. Given the time of day, the heat and the condition of the travelers, a climb up Redstone Hill would not have been inviting to either Fuller or Thoreau. It surely wasn't to me! It was easier just to stay the course of "The Post Road to Sterling." And so, I declared

---

138 As indicated on the Lancaster Map 1879. Further discussion of the road system from the early days when roads were mere footpaths traveled by Native Americans to the introduction of the rail system is presented in *A Brief History of Sterling, Massachusetts* (1931) 55.

139 This portion of the trip passes the old community called Ebenville, as indicated by a note in pencil on the back of the Walling map at the Thoreau Institute—unsigned and undated.

the Post Road as the most likely route from Lancaster to Sterling.

### *Sterling—West Sterling*

Just prior to crossing the town line into Sterling, a small-unnamed stream runs parallel to the road for about ¾ of a mile. That might well be the stream to which Thoreau refers in the essay.

> Yielding, therefore, to the heat, we strolled into the woods, and along the course of a rivulet, on whose banks we loitered, observing at our leisure the products of these new fields.[140]

Reaching the center of Sterling, the Post Road continues through town and then stretches its tentacles to the north up the hillside just beyond the town green. Then it is the steep-pitched Fitch's Hill that must be surmounted. At the top, one tentacle of the Post Road reaches westerly to Princeton (Route 62); another winds northwest along Beamon Road to the small hamlet nestled deep in the woods west of Sterling. Thoreau reminds us that it bore no natural name at the time.

It was there that Thoreau and Fuller spent the first night.[141] The Buss Tavern,[142] typical of many taverns spread over the length of the mail roads, was situated across the road from the mills. And there too, the Stillwater River, paused briefly at the dam, released its power to the grist and saw mills, and continued its flow south to the reser-

---

[140] Thoreau, *Excursions* 35.19–22.

[141] Some theorize that Thoreau followed the westbound tentacle. This would have led him to conclude the first night in the area of the Richardson Tavern. Certainly this is possible. However the trip would have been ¾ mile longer and would have required him to pass by the Buss Tavern on the second day as they made their way north along the Stillwater River and the ravine at East Princeton, as the essay indicates. They had walked a distance of just over 28 miles in approximately 14 hours—including a number of rest stops.

[142]Massachusetts Historical Commission, Inventory Form, Pottery Village. From the Sterling Historical Society.

voirs of Boylston and the Nashua River.

As I later discovered, Thoreau had a sense of humor, and it frequently blossomed in his writing. It is in West Sterling that he introduces the *Swedish inn quote*: "You will find at Trolhate excellent bread, meat, and wine, provided you bring them with you!"[143] And the joke was on me. Countless hours of research were spent in search of an inn located in the village with Swedish ties! It was eventually Professor Robert Sattelmeyer who solved the mystery as he informed me that the quote can be found in Thomas Thompson's *Travels in Sweden During the Autumn of 1812* (London: Robert Baldwin, 1813).[144] Thoreau was a consummate reader, and he especially focused on books describing travel to sites in America and around the globe. Surely he had read Thompson.

The Post Road from this small community runs north along the river to East Princeton. It is just before this village that the travelers noticed the river flowing in a deep ravine below the road.

> Our road lay along the course of the Stillwater,[145] which was brawling at the bottom of a deep ravine,[146] filled with pines and rocks, tumbling fresh from the mountains, so soon, alas! to commence its career of usefulness.[147]

---

[143] Thoreau, *Excursions* 36.26–28. Origin: Journal entry in *Journal Volume 1*, 26.2–5 dated "Jan 21st 1838."

[144] Robert Sattelmeyer. Email to author dated 7/13/06. In it, he writes of the source for Thoreau's journal entry "for Jan. 21, 1838 as being from Thomas Thomson's *Travels in Sweden during the Autumn of 1812* (London: Robert Baldwin, 1813)."

[145] Massachusetts Route 140 connects the village now known as West Sterling to East Princeton two miles to the north. The Stillwater sits west of the road.

[146] From the roadside, just before reaching East Princeton, Thoreau could see the waters in the ravine far below. Today the scene looks much as Thoreau described it. The stream can be reached from Gleason Road in the center of East Princeton. Located Lat 42.47N Long 71.83W.

[147] Thoreau, *Excursions* 37.8–12.

Today the road is called Redemption Rock Road or Massachusetts Route 140. While the river is now named Keyes Brook, the waters still thrash through the gorge as energetic as ever.

### East Princeton

Just beyond the ravine one emerges into the community of East Princeton. A small village of a few homes and even fewer shops or places of business, one passes quickly through the center where Leominster Road and Gleason Road converge upon Route 140 from the north and the south respectively. A turn down Gleason Road leads directly to the bottom of the aforementioned gulf. A half mile beyond the "center", one crosses the intersection of Route 31 and Route 140, and once again, finds himself on Beamon Road.

This paved, but narrow road surges uphill immediately, winding ever upward for about a mile whereupon it plunges down to a broad valley and an intersection with Myrick Road. The summit of Wachusett is visible across the breath of a large swamp. At last, she is close at hand.

While still in West Sterling, Thoreau wrote, "it was only four miles to the base of the mountain …."[148] This is that spot: the base of the mountain. His estimate was actually pretty good; from the Buss Tavern, it is 3.2 miles to the intersection as the crow flies; it is 4.4 miles walking distance. A glimpse of the mountain high above provides profound evidence that from this point the traveler will be gaining in elevation until the summit is reached.

Reviewing the elevations of various points about the summit, it is clear that the mountain "begins" at an elevation of approximately 900' Above Sea Level (ASL). Princeton Center (South) rests at 1,115'

[148] Thoreau, *Excursions* 37.6–7.

ASL, Wachusett Lake (North East) sits at 886' ASL, Route 62 and Gates Road (West) is at 975' ASL, and Myrick/Beamon Intersection lies 928' ASL. The topographic profile clearly indicates this verity; a visual of the area cements that fact forever.

From "the base," Myrick Road climbs quite gently and unobtrusively. Just beyond a quiet murmuring tributary of East Wachusett Brook, one of "the springs which gush out from the mountain sides,"[149] the saunterer is bound by stone fences on either side of the road; a well prepared orchard of seedlings signals Gregory Road. And here, the gentle climb is gentle no more. The pitch is severe; the walk becomes painful ... forcing one to stop, rest, and drink at the midway point.

Just before Mountain Road an old stand of sugar maples guards this eastern approach to the Wachusett Mountain State Reservation.[150] A gnarly old maple stands to one side of the narrow road; its arms are thick, bent, and twisted; its skin leathery, cracked, and tough. Nearby, other old specimens stand swollen with pride despite their weathered appearance. Together they have seen years and seasons pass, weathered winter storms, avoided the strikes of lightning, and shaded many travelers passing along their hot dusty road. Thoreau writes of the skin of the trees having been scared by the taps of the maple sugar harvest. Time has changed little; new scars disclose the annual run of sap from these hearty protectors of Wachusett.

> In due time we began to ascend the mountain, passing, first, through a grand sugar maple wood, which bore the marks of the auger, then a denser

[149] Thoreau, *Excursions* 37.19–20.

[150] Massachusetts state park of 3,000 acres managed by the Department of Conservation and Recreation.

> forest, which gradually became dwarfed, till there were no trees whatever.[151]

Close examination of the 1830 Princeton survey by Amos Merriam[152] reveals that Gregory Road bent itself about 120 degrees and headed back towards the village of Princeton along what is now Mountain Road. The continuation of Mountain Road around the mountain from Gregory Road to the north would not occur for another 40 years. In 1842, this was as close an offering to the summit as a public road would make. From here, it was a steep climb through the pastures and fields of the southeastern side of the mountain and on to higher elevations and the summit.

## *Wachusett Mountain State Reservation*

Crossing the road and entering the wood of the reservation, the Mountain House Trail beckons the saunterer ever upward. In 1793, historian Rev. Peter Whitney wrote, "upon the southerly side of this hill it may be ascended to the very top with horses, but upon the east, north and northwest, it is very steep, broken and ledgy; and many acres utterly unimprovable any way at present."[153] Thoreau might well have read this account prior to the trip; it definitely provides local geographic specifics that would have been of some practical value in planning a trip to the area.

At the turn of the century in 1800, this steep, rocky, south-facing trail was but a poorly defined footpath[154] probably used by lo-

---

151 Thoreau, *Excursions* 37.27–31.

152 Copy of Map drawn by Amos Merriam, October 1830 held by Princeton Historical Society. Merriam also conducted the survey upon which the map is based.

153 Peter Whitney, *The History of The County of Worcester, in the Commonwealth of Massachusetts,* (Worcester: Isaiah Thomas, 1793) 238.

154 Sinclair, Appendix 133.

cal residents for their own curiosity and enjoyment. It led upward through the forest from the northern extreme of a road, which ran from Princeton, passed to the east of Little Hill,[155] and on to the southeastern side of the mountain before snaking down Gregory Road to the base.

Simeon Borden used this same footpath as an access route to the summit in 1833.[156] He was there as the result of a directive from the Commonwealth in which all towns were required to submit surveys of their land areas. Wachusett provided him with a perfect site for his work. From the summit, one could labor with a clear, unimpeded view of most points in the eastern and central regions of the Commonwealth—from the Atlantic in the east to the Connecticut River in the west. It was still later, in the 1860's, that Wachusett was utilized for the Coast Survey conducted by Professor A.D. Bache as well as the Geodetic Survey and also the Massachusetts Topographical Survey Commission.[157] Wachusett, at least for this period of time in history, apparently had discovered her purpose in life. And so, the route to the summit became known as the Coast Survey Road. It was not until some time after 1859, when the Mountain House Hotel opened for commercial business, that it gained the moniker "The Mountain House Trail."

Today the path enters the reservation and splits a younger maple grove as old stone fences appear magically, crossing the steep rocky trail. Stone fences? Deep in the middle of the forest?

Princeton was incorporated in 1759 and in the course of the next

---

155 Now known as "Little Wachusett."

156 Sinclair, 14.

157 Sinclair, 15.

century, significant tracts of forested land were cleared for agricultural purposes; on the eastern side of the mountain, clearings were made for hay fields or for grazing of stock. To provide containment areas for their livestock, stone fences were constructed, there being a surplus of material about the land. And they stand proudly to this day; one can still draw a bead down the length of a stone run and find it to be perfectly straight, never wavering from the alignment set in place decades ago. In 1842 Thoreau and Fuller passed these farmlands and stone fences as Thoreau writes while on the summit: "we see the waving of trees, and hear the lowing of kine."[158]

But high on the mountain it was all virgin forest; Thoreau and Fuller crossed paths with only the trail of the deer, the fox, the skunk, and the porcupine. There, oaks and birches have taken root. And then, beyond the forest green, one sees open blue sky on *the other side.* At last, the Wachusett summit was near at hand.

## *Reaching The Summit*

From the hills of Concord, Thoreau had viewed the mountaintops to the west for years. John Winthrop, Esq., first Governor of the Colony of Massachusetts Bay saw those same mountaintops. In his journal entry dated February 7, 1631, Winthrop wrote, "On the west side of Mount Feake, they went up a very high rock, from whence they might see over all ||Neipness, || and a very high hill due west, about forty miles off, and to the N.W. the high hills by

---

[158] Thoreau, *Excursions* 38.31–31. In 1842, a significant portion of the lands in Middlesex and Worcester counties had been clear-cut for creating pastureland and land upon which to grow crops. Along with this activity came the harvesting of the trees to be used as a source of heat for the cold winter months. Borders for the fields and pastures were provided by stone fences, which exist to this day high up the southern face of Wachusett.

Merrimack, above 60 miles off."[159] The Native Americans, of course, had known of the hill for years, frequenting it as a popular hunting ground and resting place. After all these viewings, the time was now; Thoreau and Fuller would soon look back on ships at sea.

I have a vision of the Wachusett pinnacle as Thoreau and Fuller made their approach above the pines and ash—small trees, scrub brush, berries, grasses and the requisite rocks and boulders. At the highest point of land, the dilapidated tower left by the surveyors several years prior, fought its way to stand erect against the pull of age and the forces of nature. It was a battle lost well before their arrival. Summit Pond, off to the southern side of the summit, was probably not real striking either, more like a soggy, swampy bog, which the path circumvented as it twisted about the rocks to reach the summit. He either missed it or just wasn't impressed.

It is surprising too, because of its proximity to both the trail and to the summit. The pond sits adjacent to the trail and is but 20 or 30 yards from the summit. Furthermore, Thoreau had a penchant for swamps, ponds, streams, rivers, lakes, and oceans—all bodies of water. He found them to be quite alive and of great interest, writing about them in just about all the excursion essays, *Walden*, *The Maine Woods*, *A Week*, and in countless entries of his journal. For some unknown reason, this one is never mentioned in the essay.

Beyond the rim of the summit cap, the tops of trees rooted below might have danced and waved as drafts from below swept the hawk along the highway towering above the mountain.

Whitney reported that it was a "flat rock, or a ledge of rocks for

---

[159] John Winthrop, *The History of New England from 1630 to 1640,* ed. James Savage (Massachusetts Historical Society: Phelps and Farnham, 1825) 69.

some rods round, and there is a small pond of water generally upon the top of it, of two or three rods square; and where there is any earth, it is covered with blueberry bushes for acres round."[160] Years later, Thoreau describes it in a similar fashion:

> The summit consists of a few acres, destitute of trees, covered with bare rocks, interspersed with blueberry bushes, raspberries, gooseberries, strawberries, moss, and a fine wiry grass. The common yellow lily, and dwarf cornel, grow abundantly in the crevices of the rocks. This clear space, which is gently rounded, is bounded a few feet lower by a thick shrubbery of oaks, with maples, aspens, beeches, cherries, and occasionally a mountain-ash intermingled, among which we found the bright blueberries of the Solomon's Seal, and the fruit of the pyrola.[161]

Indeed, with the advent of man-made structures in 1866,[162] the stately hotels now long since destroyed,[163] and the towering communications structures of the last 25 years, it is now a much altered summit landscape.

## *The Riddle of the Heavy Tent*

In Fuller's essay, we learn that he and Thoreau shared the burden of carrying the tent throughout the journey, switching the load between their rucksacks from time to time.[164] This means that it was either heavy, bulky, or both!

---

160 Whitney, 238.

161 Thoreau, *Excursions* 38.4–15.

162 Sinclair, A129. W. G. Morse sold candy and cigars on the summit from a small retail booth.

163 Sinclair, 29. The last of the three hotels constructed on the summit burned to the ground on December 18, 1970.

164 Fuller, 3.

Now, let's closely examine the Fuller comment and the question it raises.

> The morning of the next day arrived, Mr. Thoreau and myself swallowing a good breakfast, and not heeding a threatened storm, with knapsacks filled with a day's provisions and a tent to be alternately carried by each, at about quarter of five, started.[165]

"A tent to be alternately carried by each?" How might the tent be such a burden? True, five pounds or even seven pounds can get heavy over time and distance, but … a major problem?? Worthy of mention in his essay?

Thoreau writes, "we could easily see the moon through its transparent roof as we lay."[166] And so, a conundrum of sorts: How might a tent constructed of transparent fiber lend itself to be such a burdensome object to carry?

Of the tent used during the river trip with John just two years before Wachusett,[167] a journal entry states:

> At night we lay … under a tent of drilled cotton–eight feet high and as many in diameter–which effectively defend from dampness ….[168]

And continuing later in that same journal, additional information is provided.

> From our tent here on the hillside, through that isosce-

[165] Fuller, 3.

[166] Thoreau, Excursions, 40.22–23.

[167] A report of this trip was later molded into a book-sized manuscript and published in 1849 as *A Week on the Concord and Merrimack Rivers.* Following the original publication, he made a number of subsequent changes before his death.

[168] Thoreau, *Journal Volume 1,* 126.8–10. This entry is dated "June 11th –40." A transcribed entry in *Journal Volume 2:1842–1848* (9.17–18) is dated "Sat. Aug 31st 1839." In that entry, he refers to it as "a tent of *twilled* cotton our roof–a snow white house 8 feet in height and as many in diameter." [author emphasis]. I spent considerable time researching the differences between "twilled" and "drilled," only to find that he used them interchangeably in the same phrase at different times.

les door, I see our lonely mast on the shore, ...."[169]

This tent can only be *more* formally described as a "single pole, single canvas tent" or a "conical," in other words, a "tepee." It has been used in many settings over the years; its advantage over other tents is that it is freestanding and easily transportable.[170] A tent of these dimensions yields a fabric area of approximately 12.6 square yards and a weight of approximately 6 lbs if constructed of cotton fabric. Might this have been the same tent used on Wachusett?

One thing is for certain: they would not have carried an eight-foot long center pole all the way from Concord to Wachusett. That would obviously have been selected from downed trees found in the woods. And while the conical is easily transportable, this one seemed to defy that description.

In his essay "Wild Fruits," Thoreau provides the explanation. Evidently it was not the tent that was the problem!

> Many years ago, when camping on Wachusett mountain, having carried up milk for drink because there was no water there, I picked blueberries enough through the holes in the buffalo skin on which I lay in my tent to have berries and milk for supper.[171]

Buffalo skin! Now there's a significant amount of weight, and if they each had the buffalo skin as groundcover—twice the weight!

---

[169] Thoreau, *Journal Volume 1, 134.29–30.* This entry is dated "June 21st 1840," although it begins: "Copied from pencil. "Aug. 31st 1839.– Made seven miles, and moored our boat on the west side ...."

[170] Peter Marques, Tentsmiths. [cited Oct 2005]. <http://www.tentsmiths.com/period-tents-conical-tents.html>

[171] Thoreau, *Wild Fruits: Thoreau's Rediscovered Last Manuscript,* ed. Bradley P. Dean (New York: W.W. Norton, 2000), 22. It was exactly 17 years earlier that he was on Mt. Wachusett. *Wild Fruits* was begun in the fall of 1859; it was incomplete at the time of his death in May 1862.

On Wachusett, Thoreau had apparently replicated the sleeping arrangements used on the river trip, using the same tent and the same skins. Rolling the tent and the skins together into one tight and weighty bundle unquestionably makes for a load that would have been worthy of frequent tradeoffs!

## *The Summit Campground*

One obvious question remains: where on the summit did the two pitch their tent for the night? With the construction of three summit houses since 1870 and, more recently, additional communications buildings, a fire tower, and accommodations to enhance tourism, it is difficult to specify the exact location where Thoreau and Fuller might have staked their tent, but there are clues that give us a pretty good idea as to the general location.

Notwithstanding the construction efforts, it is clear that the highest point on the mountain has remained pretty much within a small circular area since Thoreau's visit and probably well before that time. Early descriptions of the mountain as well as pictures of the summit buildings and environs taken in the late 1800s validate that assumption.[172] Today, on the northern side of the upper summit parking lot, a stubby cement post is embedded into the bedrock. Affixed upon that post rests a brass compass rose, marking the summit. As a reference point, assume that the compass rose marks the summit—both now and in 1842.

Thoreau himself indirectly informs us that the tent was not set

---

[172] Sinclair, 39–112. Furthermore, early written descriptions of the summit are remarkably consistent and in concert with what Thoreau wrote and with what we experience today. See Peter Whitney's description in *The History of the County of Worcester, in the Commonwealth of Massachusetts* and also Charles Theodore Russell's description in *The History of Princeton, Worcester County, Massachusetts.*

precisely at the summit. For upon that point sat "the foundation of a wooden observatory, which was formerly erected on the highest point, forming a rude hollow structure of stone, a dozen feet in diameter, and five or six feet in height…."[173] And following that, he writes that they "stood on the stone tower while the sun was setting…."[174] The tent was certainly resting elsewhere.

Russell described the summit as "little more than naked rock" with a covering of "meagre soil."[175] Confirming this, Thoreau described it as "bare rocks."[176] And likewise today, around the immediate circumference of the compass rose, it is rocky and insufficiently level for raising a tent until one reaches a point of approximately 40 to 50 feet away from the compass rose in a southern or eastern direction. At that distance, in 1842, tent pegs most likely could have been secured in dirt or gravely soil. The northern and western directions are discounted as locations for Thoreau's tent since they expose considerably rockier terrain with a precipitous drop off the ledge not far from the compass rose (the observatory).

Further along in the essay Thoreau gives us yet another clue that indicates the location of the tent. He writes, "it was at no time darker than twilight within the tent, and we could easily see the moon through its transparent roof as we lay…."[177] Astronomically, we know that, from the evening of the 20th through the morning of the 21st, the moon was visible between 6:19 p.m., when it rose in the south-

---

[173] Thoreau, *Excursions* 38.15–18.

[174] Thoreau, Excursions 39.32.

[175] Charles Theodore Russell, *The History of Princeton, Worcester County, Massachusetts* (Boston: Henry P. Lewis, 1838) 27.

[176] Thoreau, *Excursions*, 38.5.

[177] Thoreau, *Excursions*, 40.21–23.

east, and 3:29 a.m., when it set in the southwest. It reached a maximum altitude of only 23.3° at 10:54 p.m. positioned directly to the south of the summit.[178] It is also quite obvious that, had the tent been struck at an elevation lower than the present summit parking lot, the canopy provided by the trees would have blocked the moon from their vision.

With those facts, the tent had to have been positioned as high as possible on the mountain with an open view to the south. The essay infers that the moon was directly overhead, looking straight down upon Wachusett;[179] obviously this was not the case.

While I might have staked my tent on the hard gravel of the parking lot close to Thoreau's conical, I found only one level spot suitable for raising a tent on the whole of the summit area. On the northeastern side of the summit next to the Radio Relay Station building stands a small sapling that appears to have been tipped to its side when planted. Most likely, winds from the north drove it to that posture during its formative years. Beside the sapling is a very small and level grassy plot—just the right size for the footprint of my tent.

### *Summit Exploration*

With a pitched tent and a supper of freshly picked blueberries and milk, carried from the inn at West Sterling, it was time for exploration of the mountaintop. Indeed, as indicated by Thoreau, a ridge runs to the north; its length is about a quarter of a mile from the summit to a point at which, over a steep outbreak of rock, it drops

---

178 Astronomical positions of the moon were recreated with use of Asynx Planetarium v1.33 software. Times and positions were confirmed from data available on the U.S. Naval Observatory Website: <http://aa.usno.navy.mil/data/>.

179 Thoreau, *Excursions* 40.23.

sharply to a small stream and the lower mountain meadows.

> Before sunset, we rambled along the ridge to the north, while a hawk soared still above us. It was a place where gods might wander, so solemn and solitary, and removed from all contagion with the plain.[180]

Solitary and tranquil, the serenade is quiet to all but the sounds of nature, most noticeably, a soft summer breeze and the ever-present wood thrush. Perhaps it was an unnamed trail in 1842; perhaps he followed no trail. Today it has a name: the Old Indian Trail. In the forest, amongst the trees, the under-growth, the birds, and the rocks, little has changed over the years.

### ***Sunrise on Wachusett***

Early in the morning of the 20th, as the sun rose and set the course for the day, Thoreau took full advantage of the daylight to survey the vast landscape of the Commonwealth. Civil twilight[181] began at 3:54 a.m. with the sun coming over the horizon only 33 minutes later at 4:27 a.m.[182] This early start to the day allowed for several hours for observation and exploration before the hour of departure. Looking about, he was spellbound by what he saw from the summit.

> On every side, the eye ranged over successive circles of towns, rising one above another, like the terraces of a vineyard, till they were lost in the ho-

180 Thoreau, *Excursions* 39.21–24.

181 U.S. Naval Observatory Web Site. Definition of Civil Twilight: "The limit at which twilight illumination is sufficient, under good weather conditions, for terrestrial objects to be clearly distinguished…."<http://aa.usno.navy.mil/faq/docs/RST_defs .php>.

182 U.S. Naval Observatory Web Site. Data concerning the rise and set of astronomical bodies are available on this site. Times are Eastern Standard Time. <http://aa.usno.navy.mil /data/>.

> rizon. Wachusett is, in fact, the observatory of the state. There lay Massachusetts, spread out before us in its length and breadth, like a map. There was the level horizon, which told of the sea on the east and south, the well-known hills of New Hampshire on the north, and the misty summits of the Hoosac and Green Mountains, first made visible to us the evening before, blue and unsubstantial, like some bank of clouds which the morning wind would dissipate, on the north-west and west. These last distant ranges, on which the eye rests unwearied, commence with an abrupt boulder in the north, beyond the Connecticut, and travel southward, with three or four peaks dimly seen.[183]

Visitors through the ages might describe the picture in a like manner, but as inspirational as it reads, a visit is still required. It is truly magnificent and picturesque—in all directions. On a personal level, I have frequently gazed over the landscape with reverence as I remember that phrase … "*the observatory of the state.*"

But the story continues! Only when I became completely absorbed in the research of this essay did I look more closely at these particular words. Studying Jeremiah Lyford Hanaford's book, *History of Princeton,* I came upon several un-attributed quotes including: "rears its conical head", "to the observer from its top …,"and "the distant Hoosick and Green mountains …."[184]

Surely Hanaford's purpose was to describe the delightful scene that he viewed from the summit. But apparently an adequate description defied his literary ability. For this reason alone, I surmise that he turned to the more powerful words of another and yet . . . the words

[183] Thoreau, *Excursions* 41.28–42.9.

[184] Jeremiah Lyford Hanaford, *History of Princeton, Worcester County, Massachusetts, Civil and Ecclesiastical: from its First Settlement in 1739 to April 1852* (Worcester: C. Backingham Webb, 1852) 194.

sounded almost Thoreauvian—but not quite. He linked none of the passages to a source document or to an author! Just what is *their* source?

Soon I came upon the work of yet another Princeton historian: native son James Theodore Russell. In 1838 Russell took it upon himself to compile a history of Princeton that would include "a sketch of the present religious controversy in that place." It was but "a hasty sketch," intended for the readership of the town inhabitants, and "following, in most cases, as nearly as possible, the language of the documents and persons, from whom my facts come, I have not aimed at any embellishments." In his words, it is "a 'plain, unvarnished tale.'"[185] His words struck me as truly sincere and honest. Closer and closer … a few more lines.

Concentrating heavily upon the beginnings of the town and its ecclesiastical history, he also included a section on the "Scenery" of the countryside. Therein, he wrote of the hills, their natural beauty, and of course "the *Wachusett.*"[186] His style reminded me of Thoreau. His words reminded me of both Hanaford *and* Thoreau.

And exactly what did Russell write? "To the observer from the top, the whole state lies spread out like a map."[187] The search was over. Thoreau played with the words and came up with his version: "Wachusett is, in fact, the observatory of the state. There lay Massachusetts, spread out before us in its length and breadth, like a map."[188] Indeed he wrote it, but it was really Russell who originated

185 Russell, preface.

186 Russell, 27.

187 Russell, 27.

188 Thoreau, *Excursions* 41.31–34.

the signature phrase of the essay.

With the hour of mid-day fast approaching, it was time to depart.

## *The Dusty Road Home*

The ending of "A Walk to Wachusett" is brief and very explicit, perhaps an indication of Thoreau's physical and mental condition as they traveled the road homeward. It was a lot of miles traveled in a short period of time—for anyone. Therein, he provides us with information that allows for no mistake about the route taken; more information is provided about the third and final day of the trip than any other. From the summit, the chosen route was an exact reversal of the steps taken to reach Wachusett—until they reached the South Branch of the Nashua. There, at Lancaster Common, they turned north along the Road to Groton,[189] a country road that ran parallel to the Still River. "Leaving the Nashua, we changed our route a little, and arrived at Stillriver Village, in the western part of Harvard, just as the sun was setting."[190]

Today, we recognize this locale as a small hamlet, situated in the range of hills just south of where, in 1843, A. Bronson Alcott established his Transcendentalist experiment called Fruitlands.[191] But more importantly, we confirm through experience what Thoreau saw in late afternoon of the third day: "the prospect is beautiful, and the

---

[189] Henry S. Nourse, A.M., *History of the Town of Harvard Massachusetts: 1732–1843* (Clinton, Ma: Warren Hapgood, 1894) 13. This road had its origin as a common throughfare in 1658, described as the *"Way to the plumtrees & groten … One way: from that entervaile way donwne along all the entervailes to the Still river and towards groten on the east side of the river two rods wide. … by the recording clerk."*

[190] Thoreau, *Excursions* 45.14–16. Sunset was at 7:18 p.m.

[191] Nourse, 281. While Thoreau visited on a number of occasions, he turned down an invitation to join the experiment.

grandeur of the mountain outlines unsurpassed."[192] It is probably no small coincidence that this hill is now called Prospect Hill.

Continuing a bit farther to the small village of Harvard,[193] they spent the night and parted the next morning. Fuller moved on a few miles[194] north to the town of Groton; Thoreau turned east, and sauntered home to Concord.

Howarth surmised that the night might have been spent near the Shaker Village[195] situated in the northern section of Harvard. And while this is a possibility, a stay in the locale of the Shaker community would have required either a return to Harvard Center or, at best, a partial return, in order for Thoreau to resume travel on the most direct route to Concord, the Harvard Turnpike. Otherwise, from the Shaker community, a direct route to Concord would have been through Littleton and the Union Turnpike, now Route 2, there being no public roadway back to the Harvard Turnpike. On the other hand, a night in the center of Harvard would have lent itself to a relatively short 12-mile journey on the Harvard Turnpike[196] to reach Concord. In the end, one really cannot conclude, proof positive, as

---

[192] Thoreau, *Excursions* 45.19–21.

[193] They left the summit at noon and it was now about 8:00 p.m., Eastern Standard Time. They walked a distance of approximately 21 miles in 8 hours to reach Harvard at twilight, a pace a bit quicker than two days earlier they walked from Concord to West Sterling.

[194] For Fuller, it was an easy walk northward of about 9 miles to Groton Center. Ayer, Massachusetts, adjacent to and north of Harvard, was incorporated in 1871.

[195] William Howarth, *Walking with Thoreau* (Boston: Beacon Press, 2001) 38.

[196] Since Harvard does not, and never did abut Concord, it was necessary to transit intermediary villages: Boxborough and then South Acton in order to reach Concord. He probably took what is now Route 111 all the way to Main Street, Concord. This route was available as early as 1798. A slightly longer route would have been to take Summer Street just before West Acton, then Central Street to South Acton, thence School Street and Lawsbrook Road to West Concord. From there, Main Street would run straight to Concord and Bush.

with several other aspects of this trip, whether or not they stayed at the Shaker complex, at a home in the center, or at any other location in Harvard. In fact, it really matters not.

> We rested that night at Harvard, and the next morning, while one bent his steps to the nearer village of Groton, the other took his separate and solitary way to the peaceful meadows of Concord; … he pushed forward with new vigor, and reached the banks of the Concord before the sun had climbed many degrees into the heavens.[197]

The trip was over; Thoreau and Fuller had reached home, and so too had I. There, we three, independent of one another, yet separated by a few miles and significant time, ponder the events of our travels and reminisce.

> In the spaces of thought are the reaches of land and water, where men go and come. The landscape lies far and fair within, and the deepest thinker is the farthest travelled.[198]

---

[197] Thoreau, *Excursions* 46.4–16.

[198] Thoreau, *Excursions* 25–29.

## The Essay—"A Walk to Wachusett"

And now that I have walked Thoreau's dusty roads, studied his words of dusty roads, viewed nature's wonder from dusty roads, and slept the night by dusty roads, I feel compelled to provide commentary, remarks, and explanations as they apply specifically to the essay and to my walk. For all I have gained by this experience, it is only just that I make a fair exchange by providing some of what I have learned.

This early travel piece is focused on the westward movement of the population, from both a geographical aspect as well as an expansion of one's mind and intellectual capacity. As people moved westward, so too, did our American culture. We had been moving for years from the eastern lands of the classics to the wild of the western unknown. Thoreau, in fact, preferred deep roots of his heritage; he did travel, but the most valuable travel would be in his mind as recorded in his writings.

What Thoreau and Fuller saw and experienced runs as true today as the Concord and Nashua Rivers ran in 1842. We feel the quiet of an early morning awakening; we feel the heat of the intervale; we feel the warmth of the hostess at the inn; we feel the rush of waters from the mountain tops; we taste the berries plucked from the vine; we feel the wind rush across the summit; we experience the joy of walking the ridge; we feel the tired spirit as one departs from the mountain's summit; we muse over lessons gleaned from the experience.

Taken over several months and countless readings, my notes were meant to help me comprehend the essay as it reflected what I faced on the road. I pass them along in an effort to assist others in understanding what I missed in the beginning, what I gained by the end.

## Summary

### Beginning—Concord to Acton and Stow[199]

From Concord Thoreau often gazed over the horizon to view the mountains to the west. On October 12, 1840, a journal entry is made: "now that I am left alone, I see the blue peaks in the horizon, and am homesick." In August 4, 1841, he writes, "Here, in sight of Wachusett and these rivers and woods, my mind goes singing to itself of other themes than taxation." Thus it is that, high on the neighboring hills of Concord, Thoreau ponders the possibilities of a trip westward to Wachusett. One of his worries is that, should he visit, the mystery of the unknown mountain to the west would be no more. Gone will be dreamy visions of what lie beyond. No more will he be able to imagine the unknown and make it whatever he might wish: "thereafter no visible fairy land would exist for us."

Preparing for the journey, he draws from the classics as well as from his journal. A journal entry dated August 13, 1840 is a source of inspiration as he explains that a physical trip will expand and develop his mind: "The landscape lies fair within. The deepest and most original thinker is the farthest travelled."

Thoreau does not specify any details about the point of departure, the time, or his companion. He simply begins, and our travelers "quickly" make their way from *Bush* through the neighboring towns of Acton and Stow, their farmlands and their wooded forests.

---

[199] Thoreau, *Excursions* 29.1–32.22. This portion of the essay contains 1,003 words—18% of the essay.

**Bolton through Lancaster to W. Sterling**[200]

It is just before noontime in Bolton that Thoreau comes alive in his writing with more detailed descriptions of both what he sees and of what he is thinking. It is as if he has suddenly awakened. Reaching Bolton, he inquires of the mower in the adjacent meadow as to their location. This simple query, so often repeated by travelers today, indicates that he is beyond his geographic domain; never would this happen closer to Concord, where everything is within his grasp.

It is also at this point that the travelers realize a distinct difference in the people of the region as well as in the geography. Not only has the language changed, but the landscape is also different. They have now reached the high point separating the valley of the Concord River with that of the Nashua.

Walking in the heat of the day, they stop frequently to cool themselves. Passages from Collins and from Emerson reflect the intensity of the effort required. A reader senses it, but only a walker feels it. The power of the sun is unrelenting, and the shade of the trees and the fresh cool waters of streams they pass provide little comfort.

Soon, the shadows of late afternoon lead them to the banks of the Stillwater, in the western part of Sterling where they are greeted by "the smell of pines and roar of water." The sun disappears as a major player; the cool night air of the western hills takes center stage.

**Wachusett—On the Mountain**[201]

As expected, this portion of the essay runs the longest and is writ-

---

200 Thoreau, *Excursions* 32.23–36.36. This portion of the essay contains 1,664 words—30% of the essay.

201 Thoreau, *Excursions* 37.1–43.16. This portion of the essay contains 1,996 words—36% of the essay.

ten in the greatest detail. His words and thoughts move adroitly between what he has experienced and what he has read.

In the early morning hours of the second day, Thoreau and Fuller journey along the Stillwater to the base of the mountain and on to the summit. The six-mile walk is preparation for entrance to the heavens. The destination is at last a reality. And there, accompanied by Virgil and Wordsworth, they experience and learn the wonders of the temple called Wachusett—natural beauty, embroidered forests, valleys in the distance, night-time travelers in the sky, winds, wildlife, plants, and the heavens above.

Early on the third morning, Thoreau experiences a viewing of New England from this monadnock island that captivates his mind and his imagination. Borrowing the thoughts of Harvard College classmate, Charles T. Russell, he delivers the signature lines of the essay: "Wachusett is, in fact, the observatory of the state. There lay Massachusetts, spread out before us in its length and breadth, like a map." Embarking upon a circular journey of the horizon, near and far, he entertains thoughts of the creation of this grand scheme.

### Heading home—Summit to Concord[202]

At its zenith, the sun signals the hour of departure. A downhill journey homeward begins. Our travelers are weary physically and mentally. There is little talk; each is absorbed in thought, reflecting on the journey of the past two days.

Resting in Harvard for the night, they part ways and return to their respective homes.

---

202 Thoreau, *Excursions* 43.17–46.16. This portion of the essay contains 859 words—16% of the essay.

# A Walk to Wachusett.

The needles of the pine,
All to the west incline.[1]

CONCORD, JULY 19, 1842.

SUMMER and winter our eyes had rested on the dim outline of the mountains in our horizon,[2] to which distance and indistinctness lent a grandeur not their own, so that they served equally to interpret all the allusions of poets and travellers; whether with Homer,[3] on a spring morning, we sat down on the many-peaked Olympus, or, with Virgil,[4] and his compeers, roamed the Etrurian[5] and Thessalian hills,[6] or with Humboldt[7] measured the more modern Andes and Teneriffe. Thus we spoke our mind to them, standing on the Concord cliffs.– [8]

With frontier strength ye stand your ground,
With grand content ye circle round,
Tumultuous silence for all sound,
Ye distant nursery of rills,
Monadnock, and the Peterboro' hills;
Like some vast fleet,
Sailing through rain and sleet,
Through winter's cold and summer's heat;
Still holding on, upon your high emprise,
Until ye find a shore amid the skies;
Not skulking close to land,
With cargo contraband,
For they who sent a venture out by ye
Have set the sun to see
Their honesty.
Ships of the line, each one,
Ye to the westward run,
Always before the gale,
Under a press of sail,
With weight of metal all untold.
I seem to feel ye, in my firm seat here,
Immeasurable depth of hold,
And breadth of beam, and length of running gear.

Methinks ye take luxurious pleasure
In your novel western leisure;
So cool your brows, and freshly blue,
As Time had nought for ye to do;

For ye lie at your length,
An unappropriated strength,
Unhewn primeval timber,
For knees so stiff, for masts so limber;
The stock of which new earths are made,
One day to be our western trade,
Fit for the stanchions of a world
Which through the seas of space is hurled.

While we enjoy a lingering ray,
Ye still o'ertop the western day,
Reposing yonder, on God's croft,[9]
Like solid stacks of hay.
Edged with silver, and with gold,
The clouds hang o'er in damask[10] fold,
And with such depth of amber light
The west is dight,[11]
Where still a few rays slant,
That even heaven seems extravagant.
On the earth's edge mountains and trees
Stand as they were on air graven,[12]
Or as the vessels in a haven
Await the morning breeze.
I fancy even
Through your defiles[13] windeth the way to heaven;
And yonder still, in spite of history's page,
Linger the golden and the silver age; [14]
Upon the laboring gale
The news of future centuries is brought,
And of new dynasties of thought,
From your remotest vale.[15]

But special I remember thee,
Wachusett, who like me
Standest alone without society.
Thy far blue eye,
A remnant of the sky,
Seen through the clearing or the gorge,
Or from the windows of the forge,
Doth leaven[16] all it passes by.
Nothing is true,
But stands 'tween me and you,
Thou western pioneer,
Who know'st not shame nor fear,
By venturous spirit driven,
Under the eaves of heaven,
And canst expand thee there,
And breathe enough of air?

Upholding heaven, holding down earth,
Thy pastime from thy birth,
Not steadied by the one, nor leaning on the other;
May I approve myself thy worthy brother![17]

At length, like Rasselas,[18] and other inhabitants of happy valleys, we resolved to scale the blue wall which bound the western horizon,[19] though not without misgivings, that thereafter no visible fairy land would exist for us. But we will not leap at once to our journey's end, though near, but imitate Homer, who conducts his reader over the plain, and along the resounding sea, though it be but to the tent of Achilles.[20] In the spaces of thought are the reaches of land and water, where men go and come. The landscape lies far and fair within, and the deepest thinker is the farthest travelled.[21]

At a cool and early hour on a pleasant morning in July,[22] my companion and I passed rapidly through Acton and Stow,[23] stopping to rest and refresh us on the bank of a small stream, a tributary of the Assabet,[24] in the latter town.[25] As we traversed the cool woods of Acton, with stout staves in our hands,[26] we were cheered by the song of the red-eye, the thrushes, the phoebe, and the cuckoo; and as we passed through the open country, we inhaled the fresh scent of every field,[27] and all nature lay passive, to be viewed and travelled. Every rail, every farm-house, seen dimly in the twilight, every tinkling sound told of peace and purity, and we moved happily along the dank roads, enjoying not such privacy as the day leaves when it withdraws, but such as it has not profaned.[28] It was solitude with light, which is better than darkness. But anon, the sound of the mower's rifle[29] was heard in the fields, and this, too, mingled with the lowing of kine.

This part of our route lay through the country of hops,[30] which plant perhaps supplies the want of the vine in American scenery, and may remind the traveller of Italy, and the South of France, whether he traverses the country when the hop-fields, as then, present solid and regular masses of verdure, hanging in graceful festoons from pole to pole, the cool coverts where lurk the gales which refresh the way-farer, or in September, when the women and children, and the neighbors from far and near, are gathered to pick the hops into long troughs, or later still, when the poles stand piled in vast pyramids in the yards, or lie in heaps by the roadside.

The culture of the hop, with the processes of picking, drying in the kiln, and packing for the market, as well as the uses to which it is applied, so analogous to the culture and uses of the grape, may afford a theme for future poets.

The mower in the adjacent meadow could not tell us the name of the brook on whose banks we had rested, or whether it had any, but his younger companion, perhaps his brother, knew that it was Great Brook. Though they stood very near together in the field, the things they knew were very far apart; nor did they suspect each other's reserved knowledge, till the stranger came by.[31] In Bolton, while we rested on the rails of a cottage fence, the strains of music which issued from within, probably in compliment to us, sojourners, reminded us that thus far men were fed by the accustomed pleasures. So soon did we, wayfarers, begin to learn that man's life is rounded with the same few facts, the same simple relations everywhere, and it is vain to travel to find it new. The flowers grow more various ways than he. But coming soon to higher land,[32] which afforded a prospect of the mountains, we thought we had not travelled in vain, if it were only to hear a truer and wilder pronunciation of their names, from the lips of the inhabitants; not *Way*-tatic, *Way*-chusett, but *Wor*-tatic, *Wor*- chusett. It made us ashamed of our tame and civil pronunciation, and we looked upon them as born and bred farther west than we. Their tongues had a more generous accent than ours, as if breath was cheaper where they wagged. A countryman, who speaks but seldom, talks copiously, as it were, as his wife sets cream and cheese before you without stint.[33] Before noon we had reached the highlands overlooking the valley of Lancaster,[34] (affording the first fair and open prospect into the west,) and there, on the top of a hill,[35] in the shade of some oaks, near to where a spring bubbled out from a leaden pipe, we rested during the heat of the day, reading Virgil, and enjoying the scenery. It was such a place as one feels to be on the outside of the earth, for from it we could, in some measure, see the form and structure of the globe. There lay Wachusett, the object of our journey, lowering[36] upon us with unchanged proportions,[37] though with a less ethereal aspect than had greeted our morning gaze, while further north, in successive order, slumbered its sister mountains along the horizon.[38]

We could get no further into the Æneid than

> –atque altæ mœnia Romæ,
> –and the wall of high Rome,[39]

before we were constrained to reflect by what myriad tests a work of genius has to be tried; that Virgil, away in Rome, two thousand years off, should have to unfold his meaning, the inspiration of Italian vales, to the pilgrim on New England hills. This life so raw and modern, that so civil and ancient, and yet we read Virgil, mainly to be reminded of the identity of human nature in all ages, and by the poet's own account, we are both the children of a late age, and live equally under the reign of Jupiter.

> "He shook honey from the leaves, and removed fire,
> And stayed the wine, everywhere flowing in rivers,
> That experience, by meditating, might invent various arts
> By degrees, and seek the blade of corn in furrows,
> And strike out hidden fire from the veins of the flint."[40]

The old world stands serenely behind the new, as one mountain yonder towers behind another, more dim and distant. Rome imposes her story still upon this late generation. The very children in the school we had that morning passed, had gone through her wars, and recited her alarms, ere they had heard of the wars of neighboring Lancaster.[41] The roving eye still rests inevitably on her hills, and she still holds up the skirts of the sky on that side, and makes the past remote.

The lay of the land hereabouts is well worthy the attention of the traveller.[42] The hill on which we were resting made part of an extensive range, running from south-west to north-east, across the country, and separating the waters of the Nashua from those of the Concord, whose banks we had left in the morning, and by bearing in mind this fact, we could easily determine whither each brook was bound that crossed our path.[43] Parallel to this, and fifteen miles further west,[44] beyond the deep and broad valley in which lie Groton, Shirley, Lancaster, and Boylston, runs the Wachusett range, in the same general direction. The descent into the valley on the Nashua side, is by far, the most sudden; and a couple of miles[45] brought us to the southern branch of the Nashua,[46] a shallow but rapid stream, flowing between high and gravelly banks. But we soon learned that there were no *gelidæ valles*[47] into which we had descended, and missing the coolness of the morning air, feared it had become the sun's turn to try his power upon us.

> "The sultry sun had gained the middle sky,
> And not a tree, and not an herb was nigh,"[48]

and with melancholy pleasure we echoed the melodious plaint of our fellow-traveller, Hassan, in the desert,

> "Sad was the hour, and luckless was the day,
> When first from Schiraz' walls I bent my way."[49]

The air lay lifeless between the hills,[50] as in a seething caldron, with no leaf stirring, and instead of the fresh odor of grass and clover, with which we had before been regaled, the dry scent of every herb seemed merely medicinal. Yielding, therefore, to the heat, we strolled into the woods, and along the course of a rivulet, on whose banks we loitered, observing at our leisure the products of these new fields.[51] He who traverses the woodland paths, at this season, will have occasion to remember the small drooping bell-like flowers and slender red stem of the dogs-bane, and the coarser stem and berry of the poke,[52] which are both common in remoter and wilder scenes; and if "the sun casts such a reflecting heat from the sweet fern,"[53] as makes him faint, when he is climbing the bare hills, as they complained who first penetrated into these parts, the cool fragrance of the swamp pink restores him again, when traversing the valleys between.[54]

As we went on our way late in the afternoon, we refreshed ourselves by bathing our feet in every rill that crossed the road, and anon, as we were able to walk in the shadows of the hills,[55] recovered our morning elasticity. Passing through Sterling, we reached the banks of the Stillwater, in the western part of the town, at evening, where is a small village collected.[56] We fancied that there was already a certain western look about this place, a smell of pines and roar of water, recently confined by dams,[57] belying its name, which were exceedingly grateful. When the first inroad has been made, a few acres levelled, and a few houses erected, the forest looks wilder than ever. Left to herself, nature is always more or less civilized, and delights in a certain refinement; but where the axe has encroached upon the edge of the forest, the dead and unsightly limbs of the pine, which she had concealed with green banks of verdure, are exposed to sight. This village had, as yet, no post-office, nor any settled name. In the small villages which we entered, the villagers gazed after us, with a complacent, almost compassionate look, as if we were just making our debut in the world, at a late hour. "Nevertheless," did they seem to say, "come and study us, and learn men and manners." So is each one's world but a clearing in the forest, so much open and inclosed ground.[58] The landlord had not yet returned from the field with his men, and the cows had yet to be milked. But we remembered the inscription on the wall of the Swedish inn, "You will find at Trolhate excellent bread, meat, and wine, provided you bring them with you,"[59] and were contented. But I must confess it did somewhat disturb our pleasure, in this withdrawn spot, to have our own village newspaper handed us by our host,[60] as if the greatest charm the country offered to the traveller was the facility of communication with the town. Let it recline on its own everlasting hills, and not be looking out from their summits for some petty Boston or New York in the horizon.

At intervals we heard the murmuring of water, and the slumberous breathing of crickets throughout the night, and left the inn the next morning in the grey twilight, after it had been hallowed by the night air, and when only the innocent cows were stirring, with a kind of regret. It was only four miles to the base of the mountain,[61] and the scenery was already more picturesque. Our road lay along the course of the Stillwater,[62] which was brawling at the bottom of a deep ravine,[63] filled with pines and rocks, tumbling fresh from the mountains, so soon, alas! to commence its career of usefulness.[64] At first a cloud hung between us and the summit, but it was soon blown away. As we gathered the raspberries, which grew abundantly by the roadside, we fancied that that action was consistent with a lofty prudence, as if the traveller who ascends into a mountainous region should fortify himself by eating of such light ambrosial fruits as grow there,[65] and drinking of the springs which gush out from the mountain sides, as he gradually inhales the subtler and purer atmosphere of those elevated places, thus propitiating the mountain gods, by a sacrifice of their own fruits. The gross products of the plains and valleys are for such as dwell therein; but it seemed to us that the juices of this berry had relation to the thin air of the mountain tops.

In due time we began to ascend the mountain, passing, first, through a grand sugar maple wood,[66] which bore the marks of the auger, then a denser forest, which gradually became dwarfed, till there were no trees whatever. We at length pitched our tent on the summit.[67] It is but nineteen hundred feet above the village of Princeton,[68] and three thousand above the level of the sea; [69,70] but by this slight elevation, it is infinitely removed from the plain, and when we reached it, we felt a sense of remoteness, as if we had travelled into distant regions, to Arabia Petrea,[71] or the farthest east. A robin upon a staff, was the highest object in sight. Swallows were flying about us, and the chewink[72] and cuckoo were heard near at hand. The summit consists of a few acres,[73] destitute of trees, covered with bare rocks, interspersed with blueberry bushes, raspberries, gooseberries, strawberries, moss, and a fine wiry grass. The common yellow lily, and dwarf cornel, grow abundantly in the crevices of the rocks. This clear space, which is gently rounded, is bounded a few feet lower by a thick shrubbery of oaks, with maples, aspens, beeches, cherries, and occasionally a mountain-ash intermingled, among which we found the bright blueberries of the Solomon's Seal, and the fruit of the pyrola.[74] From the foundation of a wooden observatory, which was formerly erected on the highest point, forming a rude hollow structure of stone, a dozen feet in diameter, and five or six in height,[75] we could see Monadnock,[76] in simple grandeur, in the north-west, rising nearly a thousand feet higher, still the "far blue mountain,"[77] though with an altered profile.[78] The first day the weather was so hazy that it was in vain we endeavored to unravel the obscurity. It was like looking into the sky again, and the patches of forest here and there seemed to flit like clouds over a lower heaven. As to voyagers of an aerial Polynesia, the earth seemed like a larger island in the ether; on every side, even as low as we, the sky shutting down, like an unfathomable deep, around it. A blue Pacific island,[79] where who knows what islanders inhabit? and as we sail near its shores we see the waving of trees, and hear the lowing of kine.[80]

We read Virgil and Wordsworth in our tent, with new pleasure there, while waiting for a clearer atmosphere, nor did the weather prevent our appreciating the simple truth and beauty of Peter Bell:

"And he had lain beside his asses,
On lofty Cheviot hills."

"And he had trudged through Yorkshire dales,
Among the rocks and winding *scars*,
Where deep and low the hamlets lie
Beneath their little patch of sky,
And little lot of stars."[81]

Who knows but this hill may one day be a Helvellyn,[82] or even a Parnassus,[83] and the Muses haunt here, and other Homers frequent the neighboring plains,

Not unconcerned Wachusett rears his head
  Above the field, so late from nature won,
With patient brow reserved, as one who read
  New annuals in the history of man.[84]

The blueberries which the mountain afforded,[85] added to the milk we had brought, made our frugal supper,[86] while for entertainment, the even-song of the wood-thrush rung along the ridge. Our eyes rested on no painted ceiling, nor carpeted hall, but on skies of nature's painting, and hills and forests of her embroidery. Before sunset, we rambled along the ridge to the north, while a hawk soared still above us. It was a place where gods might wander, so solemn and solitary, and removed from all contagion with the plain. As the evening came on, the haze was condensed in vapor, and the landscape became more distinctly visible, and numerous sheets of water were brought to light,

Et jam summa procul villarum culmina fumant,
Majoresque cadunt altis de montibus umbræ."[87]

And now the tops of the villas smoke afar off,
And the shadows fall longer from the high mountains.

As we stood on the stone tower while the sun was setting, we saw the shades of night creep gradually over the valleys of the east, and the inhabitants went into their houses, and shut their doors, while the moon silently rose up, and took possession of that part.[88] And then the same scene was repeated on the west side, as far as the Connecticut and the Green Mountains, and the sun's rays fell on us two alone, of all New England men.[89]

It was the night but one before the full of the moon, so bright that we could see to read distinctly by moonlight, and in the evening strolled over the summit without danger. There was, by chance, a fire blazing on Monadnock that night, which lighted up the whole western horizon, and by making us aware of a community of mountains, made our position seem less solitary. But at length the wind drove us to the shelter of our tent, and we closed its door for the night, and fell asleep.

It was thrilling to hear the wind roar over the rocks, at intervals, when we waked, for it had grown quite cold and windy. The night was, in its elements, simple even to majesty in that bleak place–a bright moonlight and a piercing wind. It was at no time darker than twilight within the tent, and we could easily see the moon through its transparent roof as we lay; for there was the moon still above us, with Jupiter and Saturn on either hand, looking down on Wachusett,[90] and it was a satisfaction to know that they were our fellow-travellers still, as high and out of our reach as our own destiny. Truly the stars were given for a consolation to man. We should not know but our life were fated to be always grovelling, but it is permitted to behold them, and surely they are deserving of a fair destiny. We see laws which never fail, of whose failure we never conceived; and their lamps burn all the night, too, as well as all day, so rich and lavish is that nature, which can afford this superfluity of light.

The morning twilight began as soon as the moon had set,[91] and we arose and kindled our fire, whose blaze might have been seen for thirty miles around. As the day-light increased, it was remarkable how rapidly the wind went down. There was no dew on the summit, but coldness supplied its place. When the dawn had reached its prime, we enjoyed the view of a distinct horizon line, and could fancy ourselves at sea, and the distant hills the waves in the horizon, as seen from the deck of a vessel. The cherry-birds flitted around us, the nuthatch and flicker were heard among the bushes, the titmouse perched within a few feet, and the song of the wood thrush again rung along the ridge. At length we saw the sun rise up out of the sea, and shine on Massachusetts, and from this moment the atmosphere grew more and more transparent till the time of our departure, and we began to realize the extent of the view, and how the earth, in some degree, answered to the heavens in breadth, the white villages to the constellations in the sky. There was little of the sublimity and grandeur which belong to mountain scenery, but an immense landscape to ponder on a summer's day. We could see how ample and roomy is nature. As far as the eye could reach, there was little life in the landscape; the few birds that flitted past did not crowd. The travellers on the remote highways, which intersect the country on every side, had no fellow-travellers for miles, before or behind. On every side, the eye ranged over successive circles of towns, rising one above another, like the terraces of a vineyard, till they were lost in the horizon. Wachusett is, in fact, the observatory of the state. There lay Massachusetts, spread out before us in its length and breadth, like a map.[92] There was the level horizon, which told of the sea on the east and south, the well-known hills of New Hampshire on the north, and the misty summits of the Hoosac and Green Mountains, first made visible to us the evening before, blue and unsubstantial, like some bank of clouds which the morning wind would dissipate, on the north-west and west. These last distant ranges, on which the eye rests unwearied, commence with an abrupt boulder in the north, beyond the Connecticut, and travel southward, with three or four peaks dimly seen.[93] But Monadnock, rearing its masculine front in the north-west, is the grandest feature. As we beheld it we knew that it was the height of land between the two rivers, on this side the valley of the Merrimack, on that of the Connecticut, fluctuating with their blue seas of air,–these rival vales, already teeming with Yankee men along their respective streams, born to what destiny who shall tell? Watatic, and the neighboring hills in this state and in New Hampshire, are a continuation of the same elevated range on which we were standing. But that New Hampshire bluff–that promontory of a state–lowering day and night on this our state of Massachusetts, will longest haunt our dreams.

We could, at length, realize the place mountains occupy on the land, and how they come into the general scheme of the universe. When first we climb their summits, and observe their lesser irregularities, we do not give credit to the comprehensive intelligence which shaped them; but when afterward we behold their outlines in the horizon, we confess that the hand which moulded their opposite slopes, making one to balance the other, worked round a deep centre, and was privy to the plan of the universe. So is the least part of nature in its bearings referred to all space. These lesser mountain ranges, as well as the Alleghanies, run from north-east to south-west, and parallel with these mountain streams are the more fluent rivers, answering to the general direction of the coast, the bank of the great ocean stream itself. Even the clouds, with their thin bars, fall into the same direction by preference, and such even is the course of the prevailing winds, and the migration of men and birds. A mountain chain determines many things for the statesman and philosopher. The improvements of civilization rather creep along its sides than cross its summit. How often is it a barrier to prejudice and fanaticism? In passing over these heights of land, through their thin atmosphere, the follies of the plain are refined and purified; and as many species of plants do not scale their summits, so many species of folly no doubt do not cross the Alleghanies; it is only the hardy mountain plant that creeps quite over the ridge, and descends into the valley beyond.

We get a dim notion of the flight of birds, especially of such as fly high in the air, by having ascended a mountain. We can now see what landmarks mountains are to their migrations; how the Catskills and Highlands have hardly sunk to them, when Wachusett and Monadnock open a passage to the north-east–how they are guided, too, in their course by the rivers and valleys, and who knows but by the stars, as well as the mountain ranges, and not by the petty landmarks which we use. The bird whose eye takes in the Green Mountains on the one side, and the ocean on the other, need not be at a loss to find its way.[94]

At noon we descended the mountain, and having returned to the abodes of men, turned our faces to the east again; measuring our progress, from time to time, by the more ethereal hues, which the mountain assumed. Passing swiftly through Stillwater and Sterling, as with a downward impetus, we found ourselves almost at home again in the green meadows of Lancaster, so like our own Concord, for both are watered by two streams which unite near their centres, and have many other features in common. There is an unexpected refinement about this scenery; level prairies of great extent, interspersed with elms, and hop-fields, and groves of trees, give it almost a classic appearance. This, it will be remembered, was the scene of Mrs. Rowlandson's capture,[95] and of other events in the Indian wars, but from this July afternoon, and under that mild exterior, those times seemed as remote as the irruption of the Goths.[96] They were the dark age of New England. On beholding a picture of a New England village as it then appeared, with a fair open prospect, and a light on trees and river, as if it were broad noon, we find we had not thought the sun shone in those days, or that men lived in broad daylight then. We do not imagine the sun shining on hill and valley during Philip's war, nor on the war-path of Paugus,[97] or Standish,[98] or Church,[99] or Lovell,[100] with serene summer weather, but a dim twilight or night did those events transpire in. They must have fought in the shade of their own dusky deeds.

At length, as we plodded along the dusty roads, our thoughts became as dusty as they; all thought indeed stopped, thinking broke down, or proceeded only passively in a sort of rhythmical cadence of the confused material of thought, and we found ourselves mechanically repeating some familiar measure which timed with our tread; some verse of the Robin Hood ballads, for instance, which one can recommend to travel by.

> "Sweavens are swift, sayd lyttle John,
> As the wind blows over the hill;
> For if it be never so loud this night,
> To-morrow it may be still." [101]

And so it went up hill and down till a stone interrupted the line, when a new verse was chosen.

> "His shoote it was but loosely shot,
> Yet flewe not the arrowe in vaine,
> For it met one of the sheriffe's men,
> And William-a-Trent was slaine."[1012]

There is, however, this consolation to the most way-worn traveller, upon the dustiest road, that the path his feet describe is so perfectly symbolical of human life–now climbing the hills, now descending into the vales. From the summits he beholds the heavens and the horizon, from the vales he looks up to the heights again. He is treading his old lessons still, and though he may be very weary and travel-worn, it is yet sincere experience.[102]

Leaving the Nashua, we changed our route a little, and arrived at Stillriver Village, in the western part of Harvard, just as the sun was setting.[103] From this place, which lies to the northward, upon the western slope of the same range of hills, on which we had spent the noon before, in the adjacent town, the prospect is beautiful, and the grandeur of the mountain outlines unsurpassed. There was such a repose and quiet here at his hour, as if the very hill-sides were enjoying the scene, and as we passed slowly along, looking back over the country we had traversed,[104] and listening to the evening song of the robin, we could not help contrasting the equanimity of nature with the bustle and impatience of man. His words and actions presume always a crisis near at hand, but she is forever silent and unpretending.[105]

And now that we have returned to the desultory life of the plain, let us endeavor to import a little of that mountain grandeur into it. We will remember within what walls we lie, and understand that this level life too has its summit, and why from the mountain-top the deepest valleys have a tinge of blue; that there is elevation in every hour, as no part of the earth is so low that the heavens may not be seen from it, and we have only to stand on the summit of our hour to command an uninterrupted horizon.[106]

We rested that night at Harvard, and the next morning, while one bent his steps to the nearer village of Groton,[107] the other took his separate and solitary way to the peaceful meadows of Concord; but let him not forget to record the brave hospitality of a farmer and his wife, who generously entertained him at their board, though the poor wayfarer could only congratulate the one on the continuance of hayweather, and silently accept the kindness of the other. Refreshed by this instance of generosity, no less than by the substantial viands set before him, he pushed forward with new vigor, and reached the banks of the Concord before the sun had climbed many degrees into the heavens.[108]

· The text is from the Princeton University Press 2007 edition of *Excursion.*

## Essay Notes

1. *Journal, Volume 1*, 216.20–22. Entry dated "Jan 2nd 1841." While not a specific source, this entry provides an indication of the depth of Thoreau's thinking about nature even at an early time in his career.

2. From Concord, Wachusett can be found in the direction of 274.64° TN; 26.79 miles (34.3 road miles).

3. Homer (7th or 8th century B.C.) Greek author wrote of the ancient gods and their home on Mount Olympus in *The Illiad* and *The Odyssey.*

4. Virgil (70 B.C.–19 B.C.) Roman poet author of the *Eclogues*, the *Georgics*, and the *Aeneid.*

5. Ancient country, west central Italy, now forming Tuscany and portions of Umbria.

6. Hills in the northeastern region of Greece called Thessaly. Location of Mt. Olympus, home of the mythical gods.

7. Alexander von Humboldt (1769–1859), founder of modern geography. Visited and studied in the Andes, the Canary Islands (Teneriffe the largest of the Canary Islands), and other locations throughout the world.

8. Collectively, hills in Concord are called the Concord Cliffs. Krueger, in his essay "Walk to Wachusetts," indicates that it was most likely on Fairhaven Hill, situated about 1.5 miles from the center of Concord and a mile to the west of Walden Pond, that Thoreau stood, as he "recites" this poem.

9. Croft: land area owned by one having tenure and use of the land.

10. Damask: silk or linen cloth into which an elaborate pattern has been woven. The name comes from the name of the city in which it originated in the 12th century: Damascus.

11. Dight: The main sense in use was 'to dress; adorn', usually appearing as 'dressed' or 'adorned.'

12. Graven: cut or impressed into a surface.

13. Defiles: gorges, ravines, a notch or mountain pass.

14. The first two ages of humanity in Classical Mythology—the best of the traditional five ages of mankind. (~1700 ~1600 BC) <http://en.wiki pedia.org/wiki/Ages_of_Man>

15. Vale: a wide river valley, usually with a particularly wide flood plain or flat valley bottom.

16. Leaven: to raise; some leavening agents are baking powder, soda, eggs.

17. From *Henry David Thoreau: Collected Essays and Poems*. ed. Elizabeth Hall Witherell. New York: Literary Classics, 2001. p. 544. The name of the poem is "The Mountains in the Horizon."

    Robert D. Richardson Jr. *Life of the Mind*, p. 111. This poem was submitted to the Dial in the fall of 1841; it was thought to be part of plans for an anthology of his poetic work.

    The final stanza of the poem appears in *Journal 1* as a poem entitled "Wachusett." Entry dated "May 2nd 1841." 307.7–27.

18. *The History of Rasselas, Prince of Abissinia,* by Samuel Johnson. It tells the story of Rasselas, a Prince of Abyssinia, who leaves the Happy Valley of his birth with his mentor, Imlac. Travelling through Egypt they seek a happy life but are disappointed in the end. <http://en.wikipedia.org/ wiki/Rasselas>

19. Wachusett is located 274.64° TN from Concord center—positively on the *western horizon.*

20. From Homer's writings of the Trojan War in The Illiad. In *Journal Volume 1*, 55.32–35, dated Sept 7th 1838. Thoreau writes "When Homer's messengers repair to the tent of Achilles–we do not have to wonder how they get there–but step by step accompany them along the shore of the resounding sea" [no period in text.)

21. *Journal Volume 1*, 171.11–15. Date of the entry is "Aug. 13th 1840."

22. According to companion, Richard Fuller, they began on a Tuesday morning at approximately 4:45 a.m. Standard Time. He also wrote that a storm threatened, but apparently it was no reason to delay or postpone the trip.

23. The trip begins in Concord yet not a word is spilled on the specific beginning point or waypoints. This reference is the first specific notation as to the route.

24. In the colonial period, the Assabet River went by the name of North River or Elizabeth River. According to the 1830 map of Concord, these waters went by the name of North River as well as Assabet River. By 1842, it was evidently well known as the Assabet. For more information: <http://homepage.mac.com

/sfe/henry/country_not_esta/concord-river.htm>.

25. Pratt's Brook, which crosses the road in Stow, just after the boundary marking Acton–Stow. This is now in the town of Maynard.

26. Richard Fuller writes "we … soon came to a wood that lies between Concord and Stowe. Here we cut us each a cane …." A quick review of the maps reveals that land between those two towns would actually be within the boundary of the town of Acton.

27. Even today, for me, nothing is sweeter to the smell than that of a field of freshly cut hay as it lay in the field curing. I remember this from working the hayfields in the early 1950's on Christian Street in Wilder, Vermont.

28. Civil Twilight began on that day at 3:50 a.m. EST; sunrise was at 4.24 a.m. EST. Originally recorded in *Journal Volume 1*. The date of the entry is "Tuesday Aug 9th 1842." 435.22–26.

29. A whetstone for sharpening scythes. The farmers of New England retain this old English word. From Emerson *Essays: First Series*—Prudence. "If the hive be disturbed by rash and stupid hands, instead of honey, it will yield us bees. Our words and actions to be fair must be timely. A gay and pleasant sound is the whetting of the scythe in the mornings of June; yet what is more lonesome and sad than the sound of a whetstone or mower's rifle, when it is too late in the season to make hay? <http://www.emersoncentral.com/essays1.htm>

30. The farmlands of this area were well suited for the growing of hops and hop houses frequented the landscape.

31. Great Brook crosses the Great Road (Route 117) in the eastern part of Bolton in two places separated a short distance. Its destination is Elizabeth Brook, which eventually finds it way to the Assabet River.

    This vignette was originally recorded in *Journal Volume 1*. The date of the entry is "Tuesday [August] 23d 1842." 436.25–437.6.

32. They were about to ascend the hills in the western part of Bolton from which they would then begin a descent to the valley of the Nashoba.

33. In Fuller's account, he too records his thoughts on the farmers of the west, using such descriptive terms as "uncouth, "not an ideal class," "ugly," and "coarse." It is at this point in the jour-

ney that they paused to reflect upon this finding. Thoreau was much more civil and polite in projecting his thoughts on the subject.

34. Two routes through Bolton afford one such a view; one route goes over the top while a second skirts a ridge of the same hill; the hill is Watoquadoc Hill. Elevation across this ridgeline reaches 627 feet on the Old Bay Road. Wilder Road, to the North and just below the top of Watoquadoc reaches a height of only 503 feet. However, either route provides a breathtaking view.

35. The Top of Watoquadoc is actually 5 feet higher than the current road elevation and .17 miles to the northeast. But, on the whole, it is safe to say that one is "on the top of a hill."

36. To appear dark or threatening—indicating a dark sky.

37. From the highest point of Old Bay Road, it is 13.8 miles to the summit of Wachusett in a direction of 286.50° TN. "With unchanged proportions," provides an indication that they are moving closer to the destination and in a westward direction.

38. Looking towards Wachusett and gazing northward, one views a number of mountains including—in order: Gapp (1,700'), Grand Monadnock (3,105'), Watatick (1,752'), and the Watatick Range (Barrett, Kidder, Temple, Pack Monadnock, and North Pack Monadnock (1,700'–2,150'))

39. Virgil, *The Æneid*, Book I, 1–19. Most important, we learn that Aeneas is "a man apart, devoted to his mission." Aeneas's detachment from temporal and emotional concerns and his focus on the mission of founding Rome, to which Virgil alludes in the image of walls in line 12, increase as the epic progresses.

40. The Georgics, from Virgil's Works, Book First. The Georgics, the second major poem that Virgil composed. He finished it in 29 B.C.E.—poetry on the subject of agriculture, with patriotic overtones and mythological allusions. <http://www.sacred-texts.com/cla/virgil/ geo/geo00.htm>

    Perhaps Thoreau's first reference to this selection, occurs in *Journal 1*, 213.3–10: "Describing the end of the Golden Age and the commencement of the reign of Jupiter, he says– "He shook honey from the leaves …."""

41. Thoreau is much aware of the wars with the Indians during early years of Lancaster and the story of Mary Rowlandson, the heroine in the adventure. During the time of the Indian wars,

neighboring Lancaster was in fact, much larger than it was in Thoreau's time. It consisted of current towns/cities of Bolton, Hudson, Berlin, Harvard, Boxboro, Clinton, Boylston, West Boylston, Sterling and Leominster.

42. Timothy Dwight, *Travels in New England and New York.* Vol 1, (New Haven: T. Dwight, 1821) 13. He writes: "... the beautiful and magnificent scenes of nature are generally delightful to the human mind; and therefore have an obvious claim to the attention of the traveller."

43. Rev. Peter Whitney. *History of Worcester County.* (Worcester: Isaiah Thomas, 1793) 180–181. Whitney writes of the geography: "in which arise several springs, soon forming a rivulet each way. That on the northwesterly side, runs a northerly course, about a mile and a half, with a continual increase of waters, and empties into Still river, so called, within the boundaries of Lancaster. The rivulet on the southeasterly side runs an easterly course; the waters of which being augmented by small additions, become sufficient to carry mills where much business is done, at the distance of two miles from their source, except in summer months, and they are emptied into the river Assabet, about two miles southeast from Stow meetinghouse; previous to which, however, the road to Bolton crosses this stream three times." Thoreau follows the same geographical representation.

44. While Wachusett lies 13.8 miles to the west on a beeline, Thoreau mistook it as part of a wider more expansive range of hills.

45. The distance to the South Branch of the Nashua River from the top of Watoquadoc Hill is 2.6 miles and indeed, it drops suddenly, loosing 400 feet of elevation from the summit to the river.

46. There were a number of bridge crossings of the Nashua at the time. This specific reference to the South Branch indicates a crossing just below the junction of the North and South Branches. The bridge, sometimes called "Common Bridge" was on Old Common Road.

47. Latin variation meaning cool or cold valley. It is likely, in the afternoon heat that they would have been looking for cooler surroundings. At no point of the essay does Thoreau mention food, drink or nature calls.

48. William Taylor Collins, 1720–1759, *Eclogue the Second Hassan*, line 7, 8.

49. William Taylor Collins, 1720–1759, *Eclogue the Second Hassan*, line 13, 14.

50. The region of lands bounding either side of the Nashua was called the Intervale Lots and was valuable as rich farming land, obviously moist for crops and warm as it rested in the lowlands, protected from the elements.

51. An unnamed stream, possibly the same, now crosses the road shortly after leaving the intervale, just before the railroad tracks along the Sterling Road.

52. From the Dogbane Family. Spreading Dogbane, *Apocynum androsaemifolium.* Blooms from June to August in fields and along roadsides. National Audubon Society, *Field Guide to New England*, 152.

    From the Pokeweed Family, Pokeweed, *Phytolacca americana.* Blooms July to August in woodlands. National Audubon Society, *Field Guide to New Egland*, 173. Also mentioned in *Wild Fruits* on the topic of "POKE," p.132 of the Bradley P. Dean edition.

53. From R. W. Emerson Historical Discourse at Concord, on the Second Centennial Anniversary of the incorporation of the town, September 12, 1835, quoted Edward Johnson of Woburn: "Some-times passing through thickets where their hands are forced to make way for their bodies' passage, and their feet clambering over the crossed trees, which when they missed, they sunk into an uncertain bottom in water, and wade up to their knees, tumbling sometimes higher, sometimes lower. At the end of this, they meet a scorching plain, yet not so plain but that the ragged bushes scratch their legs foully, even to wearing their stockings to their bare skin in two or three hours. Some of them, having no leggins, have had the blood trickle down at every step. And in time of summer, the sun casts such a reflecting heat from the sweet fern, whose scent is very strong, that some nearly fainted.'" <http://www.rwe.org>

    This discourse also can be found in John Warner Barber's *Historical Collections,* p. 378.

    Thoreau's quote appears to be from Emerson's report since the spelling of a number of words is identical to Emerson's spelling. It appears that Emerson made the modifications from Johnson's English spelling.

54. Selection from *Journal Volume 1.* 433.15–18. The date of the entry is "Monday July 18th 1842"—the day before the journey began.

55. The Post Road or the Sterling Road skirted the northern flank of Redstone Hill. On a sunny day, it would have provided shade while on the Northeast side. Gaining on the center of Sterling, the Post Road runs parallel to a ravine that would have provided cool shade and possible running waters.

56. The Stillwater River lies to the northwest of Sterling in the hills approaching Princeton and Mount Wachusett. It is reached by following the Post Road to Westminster.

57. Dams on the Stillwater at West Sterling were built for use by nearby sawmills and later the pottery industry that frequented the small community. Later, this village was referred to as Pottery Village.

58. Thoreau, *Journal Volume 1: 1837–1844*, 45.20–29. Journal entry while on a trip to Maine. Dateline "Portland to Bath–via Brunswick-Bath to Brunswick-May 5th. – –"

59. Henrik Otterberg, University of Gothenburg, Sweden wrote that this line comes from an anecdote in Thoreau's journal entry for 21 January 1838. *Journal, Volume 1*, 26.2–5. Entry dated "Jan 21st 1838"

    Professor Robert Sattelmeyer, Georgia State University, wrote that the source for that journal entry was Thomas Thompson's *Travels in Sweden During the Autumn of 1812* (London: Robert Baldwin, 1813).

60. It was common for stagecoaches, carrying passengers or mail, to drop editions of newspapers from major cities (*Boston Post, Boston Transcript*). In this case, perhaps the paper was the well-known *Concord Freeman.*

61. Depending upon what is defined to be the "base of the mountain" this is a good estimate. I use the intersection of Beamon Road and Myrick Road as the "Base". The road walking distance to that point is 4.4 miles from the Buss Tavern in West Sterling. The summit is 6.4 miles from the tavern by way of the road.

62. The Stillwater, from the village now known as West Sterling, runs northward along Route 140 to East Princeton.

63. The road rises along a steep incline, giving way to the river being

"at the bottom of a deep ravine." The bottom of the ravine can be reached from Gleason Road in the center of East Princeton.

64. Surely this comment refers to the dams built to provide energy for the grist and saw mills situated just across the street from the Buss Tavern.

65. *Wild Fruits*, on the High Blackberry, p. 71. "Along the up-country roads in New Hampshire and Maine they seem to be mainly confined to the roadside, growing in its wash ... as if expressly for the foot traveler, who ... gathers vigor to renew his journey."

66. The final public road of the journey is Gregory Road. At the intersection with Mountain Road just opposite the property of the State Reservation, there stand several old sugar maples. Clearly, they have scars from the bit of the sugar drill. Even unto this day, sap is bled from these strong pillars annually as the farmer produces yet another delicacy from nature. It is but a mile to the summit from the trailhead! From the maple bush to the summit one passes a dense forest, smaller trees and finally the summit.

67. Location: 42°29'20"N, 71°53'14"W

68. The village of Princeton is not on the route taken by Thoreau. It would have been possible although it was a bit off the direct route to the summit. This reference to the village is probably because most of the mountain area lies within the boundary of Princeton.

69. Officially the elevation is 2,006 ft above sea level and approximately 900 ft above Princeton center.

70. Thoreau probably obtained these facts from either of two sources. The first by John Warner Barber written in 1839: "It is a little more than 3,000 feet above the level of the sea, and rises, without any steep ascent, about 1,900 feet higher than the surrounding country." [Barber, 599] The second, by Charles Theodore Russell, was written in 1838: "The mountain rears its conical heat 1900 feet higher, making its total elevation above Massachusetts Bay, 3000 feet." [Russell, 27]

71. Arabia Petraea, also called Provincia Arabia or simply Arabia, was a province of the Roman Empire beginning in the second century.

    *Journal Volume 1*, 386.25–28. Entry dated "March 21st 1842." While not a direct quote, this reference reflects his thoughts about the mid-eastern lands around the globe.

72. Eastern Towhee

73. Thoreau's estimate is overstated. An estimate of today's summit (the top parking lot area of the Ranger Tower and the Radio Relay Towers) is .75 acres.

74. Also written *Pirola*; a genus of evergreen herbaceous plants in the family Ericaceae, also called wintergreen.

75. J.L. Hanaford, *History of Princeton*, p 194. Here, Hanaford uses the identical description as written by Peter Whitney in his book, *History of Worcester County*, p 238. Both refer to the flat rock or small ledge of rock. Hanaford adds mention of the construction of an octagonal tower, approximately 30 feet in height, in 1828. He adds that by 1852, when his book was published, the tower was shattered and of little use. This is Thoreau's "stone tower" of which he writes in *Excursions*, 39.32.

76. Bearing 335.51° TN, 27.43 miles distant. The elevation of Mount Monadnock is 3,165 ft. It is the most prominent feature of the horizon to the west.

77. The only reference to this quote that I could find was found in the Cambridge University Magazine, unknown author, *Prince Seraphim, or the Fallen Angel*, Vol. 2, no. 1. 1843. And certainly, there is insufficient reason to believe that Thoreau obtained the phrase from this source. This particular volume was published after "A Walk to Wachusett."

    In *Journal 1*, 169.13–15 (entry dated "Aug 8th 1840"), writing about the 1839 trip on the Merrimack River, Thoreau declares, "Every sweep of the oar brings us nearer to "the far blue mountain." This is obviously a phrase, which because of its reality in nature and his experience looking afar from hilltops, held great meaning for Thoreau. On the Merrimack, the phrase refers to Uncannunuc Mountain; on Wachusett, it refers to Mount Monadnock.

    In an email dated 8/04/08, Dr. Joseph Moldenhauer, editor of the Princeton University Press 2007 edition of *Excursions*, wrote that this phrase is one of the ten quotations or references in *Excursions* for which he was not able to identify a source. See *Excursions*, Textual Introduction p. 376.

78. A simple fact of parallax. Seeing an irregular object from a changing angle provides a different silhouette from each angle of sight. On Watoquadoc Hill, Monadnock was viewed from 38

miles distant in a direction of 320° TN; it is now 28 miles distant on a bearing of 336° TN.

79. *Journal Volume 1*, 436.4–6. Dated "Tuesday August 9th 1842." Interestingly, he has changed the location from "a blue *Atlantic* island" in the journal to "a blue *Pacific* island" in the essay.

80. Pastures and open fields were quite common on the South and Eastern sides of the mountain. Just a short distance into the woods on the Mountain House Trail several stone fences still remain, a reminder of what once was. They were erected as boundaries for pastures and fields, which stretched far up the sides of the mountain.

81. William Wordsworth, *Peter Bell, A Tale*, line 224–230.

82. Third highest peak in England; written about by Wordsworth.

83. Mountain in Greek Mythology that served as home of the Muses.

84. Thoreau, *Collected Essays and Poems*, New York: Literary Classics of the United States, Inc., 580. This poem is untitled.

85. Wachusett blueberries were a very popular product of the mountain throughout the early days, especially when the hotel business thrived on and about the region. Word has come down that Boston's posh hotels served blueberries from the hillside when they were in-season.

86. *Wild Fruits.* "Many years ago, when camping on Wachusett mountain, having carried up milk for drink because there was no water there, I picked blueberries enough through the holes in the buffalo skin on which I lay in my tent to have berries and milk for supper." p 22.

87. Virgil; *Ecloque*, (I, 84).

88. The Sun officially set at 7:19 p.m. while the moon rose at 6:19 p.m. The moon appeared in the Southeast and finally set in the morning in the Southwest at 3:29 a.m. (7/21/1842).

89. A veiled indication that this piece was written for his brother John, is found in A *Week*, Princeton UP edition, 1980. On page 445, in the Historical Introduction, the editor cites a rendition of this selection from the Nature Album draft of "A Walk to Wachusett." "And then the same *tragedy* was repeated on the west side, as far as the Connecticut and the Green Mountains, and the suns rays fell on us two alone, of all New England men. *And we had only to rise a little higher that the sun might never set to us.*"

90. On this night the moon reached its maximum altitude of just over 23 degrees at approximately 10:52 p.m. The observation would be made directly to the south.

91. Thoreau clearly has his observations in order. Civil Twilight began at 3:55 a.m., while the moon set just 26 minutes before at 3:29 a.m.

92. These two sentences are derived from Russell's *History of Princeton*, which was written in 1838. "To the observer from its top, the whole state lies spread out like a map." p 27.

    Further along in Russell's descriptive narrative on the same page, he writes of "the harbor . . . the Monadnock . . . the distant Hoosick and Green mountains"—clearly another phrase used by Thoreau.

93. Attempting to reconstruct this picture, I scanned the horizon west of Monadnock and out beyond the Connecticut into the Green Mountains. There, dim peaks do appear. And as your eyes turn southward, a line of sight might include Stratton Mountain (3,940'), Bromley Mountain (3,229'), Mount Snow (3,552'), and Glastenbury Mountain (3,698'), all in the Green Mountains, and then Mount Greylock (3,490') in the Berkshire range. All are in the range of 60–70 miles distant. However, to view them, one must have a very clear day, and even then, being difficult to differentiate, they may appear simply as "peaks dimly seen."

94. I am not sure how much of a "dim notion" he had for the flight of birds; it would appear that his "notion" was rather sound as we might expect from the author of "Natural History of Massachusetts," written before "A Walk to Wachusett." Today, as has been the case for decades, if not centuries, the pathway of autumn hawk migrations runs almost directly over Wachusett. This makes Wachusett an especially popular site for birdwatchers to view this spectacular annual activity.

95. Mary Rowlandson (1636–1711); kidnapped with her three children in 1676 by the Narragansett Indians during King Phillip's War with the colonists of central Massachusetts. Later she was freed at Redemption Rock located at the foot of Mount Wachusett.

96. An East Germanic tribe that originated in Scandinavia (specifically Gotland and Götaland). They migrated southwards and conquered parts of the Roman empire.

97. Indian chief Paugus was a member of the Pequaket tribe. Killed in 1725.

98. Captain Miles Standish, 1854–1656

99. Author Thomas Church, esq., Indian Wars from 1075 to 1704

100. Captain John Lovell (or Lovewell) well-known Indian fighter, leader of a company of men who attacked Indian villages along the New England frontier.

101. Joseph Ritson (1752–1803), Robin Hood and Guy of Gisborne, 15th Century. Site:<http://www.sacred-texts.com/neu/eng/boeb/boeb 17.htm.>

102. *Journal Volume 1*, 435.28–436.1. Entry dated "Monday Aug. 8th 1842."

103. 7:18 p.m. Since they left the summit at noon, they reached "this prospect" (about 20 miles) in just over 7 hours. The total distance to Harvard was approximately 21miles.

104. They would have been somewhere on Prospect Hill where the view is excellent across the valley of the Nashoba to Wachusett and its sister mountains to the north. This location is about 3.5 miles north of Watoquadoc Hill in Bolton.

105. *Journal Volume 1*, 303.26–28. Entry dated "April 25th 1841."

106. *Journal Volume 1*, 266.12–17. Entry dated "Feb. 15th 1841."

107. The distance for Fuller was a bit less than 9 miles over easy terrain.

108. From Harvard to the banks of the Concord, via the Harvard Turnpike, the distance is just over 12 miles. In *Journal Volume 2, 377.19–378.17,* Thoreau summarized the final paragraphs of the essay. It appears in the chapter titled "Winter 1846–1847."

# Final Thoughts

A walk from Concord to the summit of Wachusett Mountain as a companion of Henry David Thoreau is pure imagination, straight from the page—until you physically take that journey. I claim that pleasure. On that trip I traveled the globe; I traveled in ages past; I gazed beyond the horizon to celestial space, and there, imagined travel to other globes; I met wonderful people; I learned from brilliant teachers. More than an accumulation of destinations and people, I, too, found Nature at rest and in storm; I walked amongst things animate and inanimate. And I loved them all.

Having reached my destination, I returned home richer for my travels. And I remembered what both Thoreau and Collingswood had told me: while "weary and travel worn, it is yet sincere experience."[203]

> And now that we have returned to the desultory life of the plain, let us endeavor to import a little of that mountain grandeur into it. We will remember within what walls we lie, and understand that this level life too has its summit, and why from the mountain-top the deepest valleys have a tinge of blue; that there is elevation in every hour, as no part of the earth is so low that the heavens may not be seen from it, and we have only to stand on the summit of our hour to command an uninterrupted horizon.[204]

[203] Thoreau, *Excursions* 45.12–13.

[204] Thoreau, *Excursions* 45.30–46.3.

# Appendix—Illustrations

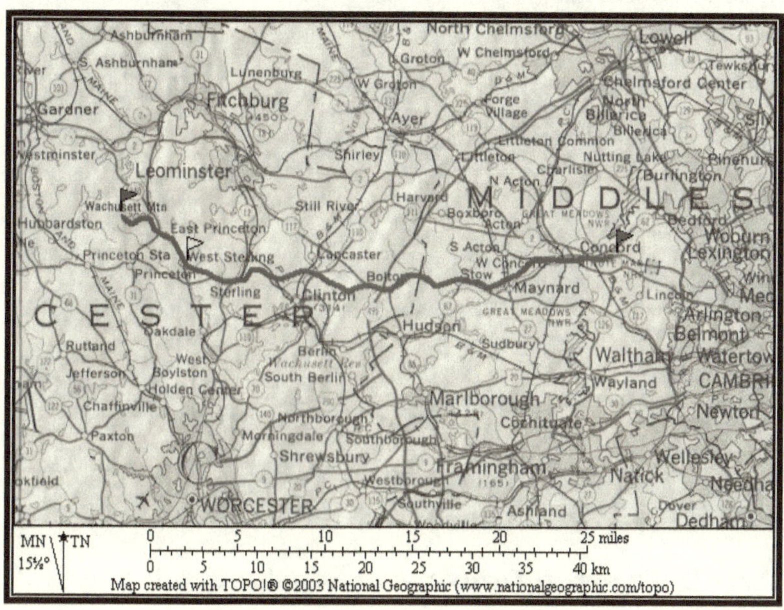


**Plate 1. Walking to Wachusett**

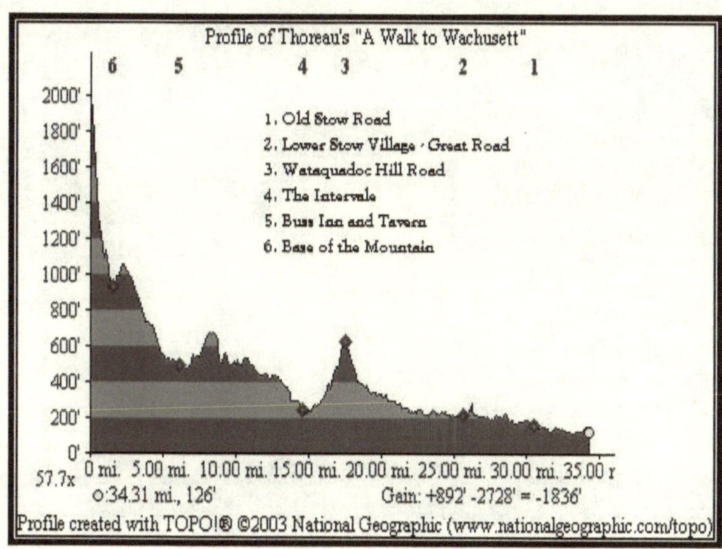


**Plate 2. Profile and Key Landmarks**

Plate 3. ***Emerson House***—"At a cool and early hour …."

**Plate 4. Concord—"on a pleasant morning in July …."**

**Plate 5. The Sudbury—"every tinkling sound told of peace and purity …."**

**Plate 6. Sunrise West Concord**

**Plate 7. "we passed through the open country …."**

**Plate 8. "we inhaled the fresh scent of every field …."**

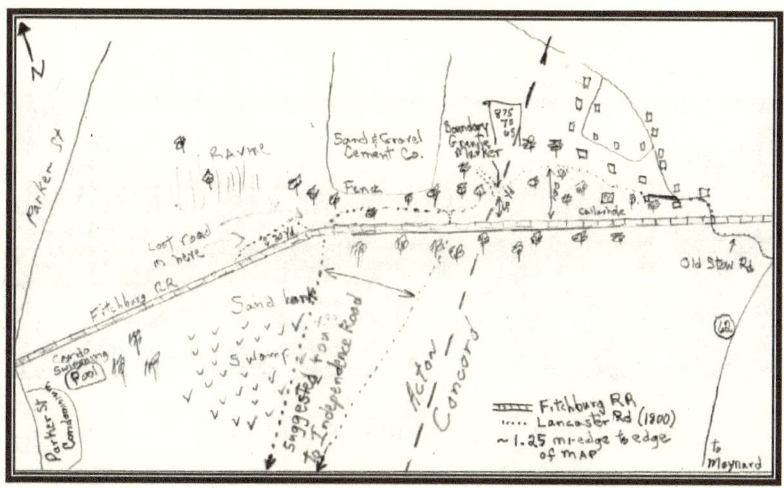


**Plate 9. "Old Road to Stow"—map by the Author**

**Plate 10. "All nature lay passive, to be viewed and traveled."**

**Plate 11. "Solitude with light"**

**Plate 12. The Intervale—"the sun's turn to try his power upon us."**

**Plate 13. "The fresh odor of grass and clover …."**

**Plate 14. "Passing through Sterling …."**

**Plate 15. Cellar Hole—The Buss Tavern**

**Plate 16. "Passing first, through a grand sugar maple wood …."**

**Plate 17. "The observatory of the state."**

**Plate 18. Summit Compass Rose and Communications Tower**

**Plate 19. "At noon we descended the mountain ...."**

**Plate 20. The Dusty Road Home—"weary and travel-worn ...."**

# Appendix—Textual Sources

"Ask and it will be given to you; seek and you will find; knock and the door will be opened to you."[205] Therein lies the thrill of the quest, a surprise nugget, an unknown sighting, a breakthrough, an invention, and victory known only to the pioneer who dares ask questions and seek answers.

Unquestionably, this adventure has led to several such victorious moments as I discovered the route of Thoreau and Fuller. But, equally as exciting was the unearthing of Thoreau's sources.

Innocently and perhaps naively, I thought this to be an essay which, upon completion of the journey, Thoreau simply sat down and wrote. But it turns out to have been far more complex an endeavor than I had imagined. The journey was only the framework for the essay. To reach its potential and to satisfy his passion for writing, he had to fill in the blanks with other material, whether newly crafted, from his journal, or from the writings of others.

My first discovery was the fact that these additions even existed. Beyond that, I had to satisfy my own passion; I was forced to search for their origins. My work would be both unfinished and imperfect should I cut short the effort.

It was in discovering the sources of these components of the essay that I have received my greatest joy and delight. But, as soon as one was discovered, yet another would be flushed from the bush, and a new hunt would continue down another path.

Some phrases are direct quotes; others are paraphrased. And

---

[205] Mathew 7: 7–8 (New International Version). "Verse 7: Ask and it will be given to you; seek and you will find; knock and the door will be opened to you. Verse 8: For everyone who asks receives; he who seeks finds; and to him who knocks, the door will be opened."

many, as it turns out, are from his own writings, most notably his *Journal.* But in only a few cases did he indicate the source of his quotes or the phrase in question.

The table below provides a matrix of those findings. Some are obvious; others may only indicate a fleeting connection. Whether the source line was the origin or only a related thought not connected to his final word, we might never know.

Each phrase from "A Walk to Wachusett" is cited as it appears in the 2007 edition of *Excursions*, published by Princeton University Press (page.line, in which the line number is literal by count). Most entries can be found in the textual apparatus of that same volume.

## "A Walk to Wachusett"—Source Matrix

| "A Walk to Wachusett" | Source / Statement |
|---|---|
| ***Excursions*, Princeton UP, 2007. 28.2–3**<br><br>The needles of the pine,<br>All to the west incline. | ***Journal, Volume 1*, 216.17–19.** Entry dated "Jan 2nd 1841." While not an exact source, this entry provides an indication of the depth of Thoreau's thinking about nature even at an early time in his career.<br><br>"Every needle of the white pine trembles distinctly in the breeze, which on the sunny side give the whole tree a shimmering seething aspect." |
| ***Excursions*, 29.16**<br><br>With frontier strength<br>ye stand your ground,<br>With grand content ye circle round,<br>Tumultuous silence for all sound,<br>. . . . | ***Henry David Thoreau: Collected Essays and Poems***, Ed. Elizabeth Hall Witherell. New York: Literary Classics, 2001. Poem: "Mountains in the Horizon" Final section is a stand-alone poem from ***Journal, Volume 1*, 307.7–25**. dated "May 2nd 1841"<br>"With frontier strength ye stand your ground –<br>With grand content ye circle round – ...."<br>[More lines and in a different order than found in "A Walk to Wachusett"] |
| ***Excursions*, 31.22–25**<br><br>But we will not leap at once to our journey's end, though near, but imitate Homer, who conducts his reader over the plain and along the resounding sea, though it be but to the tent of Achilles. | ***Journal, Volume 1*, 55.28–31.** Entry dated "Sept 7th 1838."<br>"When Homer's messengers repair to the tent of Achilles–we do not have to wonder how they get there–but step by step accompany them along the shore of the resounding sea" [no period in text.) |
| ***Excursions*, 31.25–29**<br><br>In the spaces of thought are the reaches of land and water, where men go and come. The landscape lies far and fair within, and the deepest thinker is the farthest travelled. | ***Journal, Volume 1*, 171.10–15.** Entry dated "Aug. 13th 1840." Thoreau found the phrase "to descry new lands" from either Milton in *Paradise Lost, Book I* or from William Hazlitt's *Why Distant Objects Please*, which may be found in *Table Talk: Essays on Men and Manners* (1822).<br>"To travel and "descry new lands" is to think new thoughts and have new imaginings. In the spaces of thought are the reaches of land and water over which men go and come. The landscape lies fair within. The deepest and most original thinker is the farthest travelled." |

| "A Walk to Wachusett" | Source / Statement |
|---|---|
| ***Excursions*, 32.3–7**<br><br>… and we moved happily along the dank roads, enjoying not such privacy as the day leaves when it withdraws, but such as it has not profaned. | ***Journal Volume 1*, 435.22–26.** Entry dated "Monday Aug. 8th 1842."<br><br>"In the morning you see the distinct form of every tree and creep happily along the dank roads like some new creation of her exuberance. … Not such privacy as the day leaves but such as the day has not prophaned." |
| ***Excursions*, 32.28–35**<br><br>The mower in the adjacent meadow could not tell us the name of the brook on whose banks we had rested, or whether it had any, but his younger companion, perhaps his brother, knew that it was Great Brook. Though they stood very near together in the field, the things they knew were very far apart; nor did they suspect each other's reserved knowledge, till the stranger came by. | ***Journal Volume 1*, 436.25–437.2.** Entry dated "Tuesday 23d 1842."<br><br>"The man in the field could not tell us the name of the brook only hat it was *the* brook–but the young man going to his work knew that it was Great Brook– … They shall not even suspect each others reserved knowledge till the stranger comes by." |
| ***Excursions*, 33.7–15**<br><br>But coming soon to higher land, which afforded a prospect of the mountains, we thought we had not traveled in vain, if it were only to hear a truer and wilder pronunciation of their names, from the lips of the inhabitants; not *Way*-tatic, *Way*-chusett, but *Wor*-tatic, *Wor*- chusett. It made us ashamed of our tame and civil pronunciation, and we looked upon them as born and bred farther west than we. Their tongues had a more generous accent than ours, as if breath was cheaper where it wagged. | Timothy Dwight, ***Travel in New England and New York. Volume IV***<br>I am not sure that this idea was received upon reading Dwight, but the selection in *A Walk* always struck me as an unusual argument, yet one that is quite believable. I was surprised to come upon the same position when I read Dwight.<br><br>Volume IV includes a somewhat extensive section on the differences in language between the citizens of England and those of New England. Dwight refers to differences in the pronunciation of a number of words. His intent was to prove that America's citizens were no less worthy than people far to the east in England and other European countries. |

| "A Walk to Wachusett" | Source / Statement |
| --- | --- |
| ***Excursions*, 34.25–26**<br><br>The lay of the land hereabouts is well worthy the attention of the traveller. | Timothy Dwight, ***Travels in New England and New York*., Volume 1,** (New Haven: T. Dwight, 1821) 13.<br><br>"… the beautiful and magnificent scenes of nature are generally delightful to the human mind; and therefore have an obvious claim to the attention of the traveller." |
| ***Excursions*, 34.27–32**<br><br>The hill on which we were resting makes part of an extensive range, running from south-west to north-east, across the country, and separating the waters of the Nashua from those of the Concord, whose banks we had left in the morning, and by bearing in mind this fact, we could easily determine whither each brook was bound that crossed our path. | Rev. Peter Whitney. ***History of Worcester County*.** (Worcester: Isaiah Thomas, 1793) 180–181.<br><br>"… in which arise several springs, soon forming a rivulet each way. That on the northwesterly side, runs a northerly course, a bout a mile and a half, with a continual increase of waters, and empties into Still river, so called, within the boundaries of Lancaster. The rivulet on the southeasterly side runs an easterly course; the waters of which being augmented by small additions, become sufficient to carry mills where much business is done, at the distance of two miles from their source, except in summer months, and they are emptied into the river Assabet, about two miles southeast from Stow meetinghouse; previous to which, however, the road to Bolton crosses this stream three times." |
| ***Excursions*, 35.27–32**<br><br>… and if "the sun casts such a reflecting heat from the sweet fern," as makes him faint, when he is climbing the bare hills, as they complained who first penetrated into these parts, the cool fragrance of the swamp pink restores him again, when traversing the valleys between. | From RW Emerson's **Historical Discourse at Concord**, given on the Second Centennial Anniversary of the Incorporation of the town, September 12, 1835, in which he quoted Edward Johnson of Woburn and his piece "Wonder-working Providence" (1653). This quote is entirely Johnson's as modified by Emerson for spelling and grammar.<br><http://www.rwe.org><br>"Some-times passing through thickets where their hands are forced to make way for their bodies' passage, and their feet clambering over the crossed trees, which when they missed, they sunk into an |

| "A Walk to Wachusett" | Source / Statement |
|---|---|
| | uncertain bottom in water, and wade up to their knees, tumbling sometimes higher, sometimes lower. At the end of this, they meet a scorching plain, yet not so plain but that the ragged bushes scratch their legs foully, even to wearing their stockings to their bare skin in two or three hours. Some of them, having no leggins, have had the blood trickle down at every step. And in time of summer, the sun casts such a reflecting heat from the sweet fern, whose scent is very strong, that some nearly fainted."<br><br>The quote included in *Excursions* appears to be of Emerson since the spellings have been modified from Johnson's English spelling and that is the version used by Thoreau … unless Thoreau made the exact same spelling changes.<br><br>It also appears in John Warner Barber. ***Historical Collections,*** 378.<br><br>Also, see Thoreau's Journal entry for "Monday July 18th 1842." ***Journal Volume 1*, 433.18–28.** Note: this is the day before the journey to Wachusett took place. |
| ***Excursions*, 36.16–23**<br><br>In the small villages which we entered, the villagers gazed after us, with a complacent, almost compassionate look, as if we were just making our debut in the world, at a late hour. "Nevertheless," did they seem to say, "come and study us, and learn men and manners." So is each one's world but a clearing in the forest, so much open and inclosed ground. | ***Journal, Volume 1*, 44.23–30.** Entry dated "Portland to Bath–via Brunswick–Bath to Brunswick–May 5th. – –" Thoreau was on a journey to Maine that took place between May 3rd and May 17th 1838.<br><br>"Each one's world is but a clearing in the forest, so much open and inclosed ground. When the mail coach rumbles into one of these, the villagers gaze after you with a compassionate look, as much as to say: "where have you been all this time, that you make your *début* in the world at this late hour? Nevertheless, here we are; come and study us, that you may learn men and manners." |

| "A Walk to Wachusett" | Source / Statement |
|---|---|
| ***Excursions***, **36.23–26**<br><br>The landlord had not yet returned from the field with his men, and the cows had yet to be milked. But we remembered the inscription on the wall of the Swedish inn, "You will find at Trolhate excellent bread, meat, and wine, provided you bring them with you," and were contented. | ***Journal, Volume 1***, **26.2–5.** Entry dated "Jan 21st 1838"<br><br>"This was the pith of the inscription on the wall of the Swedish inn–"You will find at Trolhate excellent bread, meat and wine, provided you being them with you!"<br><br>Professor Robert Sattelmeyer wrote in an e-mail that the source for that journal entry was Thomas Thompson's ***Travels in Sweden during the Autumn of 1812*** (London: Robert Baldwin, 1813).<br><br>"The English remarks were usually sarcastic, and often improperly so. I shall quote one which struck me on account of its originality. It was as follows: 'You will find at Trollhätte excellent wine, meat, bread, and indeed every thing, *provided you bring it along with you*.'" —*Travels in Sweden.* Italics by Thomson. |
| ***Excursions***, **37.31–35**<br><br>We at length pitched our tent on the summit. It is but nineteen hundred feet above the village of Princeton, and three thousand above the level of the sea; but by this slight elevation, it is infinitely removed from the plain …. | Charles Theodore Russell, ***The History of Princeton*** (Boston: Henry P. Lewis, 1838) 27.<br><br>"The general elevation of the circumjacent country is 1100 feet. The mountain rears its conical head 1900 feet higher, making its total elevation above Massachusetts Bay, 3000 feet." – Russell<br><br>Or perhaps …<br><br>John Warner Barber, ***Historical Collections*** (Worcester: Dorr, Howland, 1839) 599.<br><br>"It is a little more than 3,000 feet above the level of the sea, and rises, without any very steep ascent, about 1,900 feet higher than the surrounding country." –Barber<br><br>Or did Barber get his facts from Russell? |

| "A Walk to Wachusett" | Source / Statement |
|---|---|
| ***Excursions*, 37.31–38.1**<br>… and when we reached it, we felt a sense of remoteness, as if we had travelled into distant regions, to Arabia Petræa, or the farthest east. | ***Journal Volume 1*, 386.25–28.** Entry dated "March 21st 1842." While not a quote, this reference reflects his thoughts about the mid-eastern lands.<br><br>"When I look back eastward over the world it seems to be all in repose Arabia–Persia–Hindostan–are the land of contemplation. Those eastern nations have perfected the luxury of idleness." |
| ***Excursions*, 38.18–21**<br><br>… we could see Monadnock, in simple grandeur, in the north-west, rising nearly a thousand feet higher, still the "far blue mountain," though with an altered profile. | ***Journal Volume 1*, 169.9–15.** Entry dated "Aug. 8th 1840."<br><br>"We hear it muttered of some village far up amid the hills, and look to our chart and guide book to learn of its mountains, and caves, and rivers. For the livelong day there skirts the horizon the dark blue outline of Crotched Mountain, in Goffstown, as we are told. Every sweep of the oar brings us nearer to "the far blue mountain.""<br><br>From this entry, it is clear that Thoreau frequently used maps and guidebooks for reference. On the trip up the Concord and Merrimack Rivers, the journey to which he is referring in this journal entry, he carried and consulted Hayward's *The New England Gazetteer.* "The far blue mountain" is a reference to Uncanoonuc Mountain in New Hampshire.<br><br>The phrase "far blue mountain" is also found in Cambridge University Magazine, unknown author, *Prince Seraphim, or the Fallen Angel,* Vol. 2, no. 1. 1843. |
| ***Excursions*, 38.29–32**<br><br>A blue Pacific island, where who knows what islanders inhabit? and as we sail near its shores we see the waving of trees, and hear the lowing of kine. | ***Journal Volume 1*, 436.4–6.** Entry dated "Tuesday Aug 9th 1842" after 12 pages noted as deleted.<br><br>"A blue Atlantic island where who knows what islanders inhabit. While we sail near its shores we see the waving of the trees and hear the lowing kine." |

| "A Walk to Wachusett" | Source / Statement |
|---|---|
| ***Excursions*, 39.11–14**<br><br>Not unconcerned Wachusett rears his head<br>Above the field, so late from nature won,<br>With patient brow reserved, as one who read<br>New annuals in the history of man. | Untitled poem by Thoreau in *Collected Essays and Poems* –Literary Classics of the U.S.<br><br>"Not unconcerned Wachusett rears his head<br>Above the field, so late from nature won,<br>With patient brow reserved, as one who read<br>New annuals in the history of man …" |
| ***Excursions*, 39.11**<br>Not unconcerned Wachusett rears his head…." | Charles Theodore Russell. ***The History of Princeton*** (Boston: Henry P. Lewis, 1838), 27.<br><br>"The mountain rears its conical head 1900 feet higher …." |
| ***Excursions*, 41.14–17**<br><br>At length we saw the sun rise up out of the sea, and shine on Massachusetts, and from this moment the atmosphere grew more and more transparent till the time of our departure …." | ***Journal Volume 1*, 193.12–15.** Entry dated "Nov. 1st 1840."<br><br>"I thought that the sun of our love should have risen as noiselessly as the sun out of the sea, and we sailors have found ourselves steering between the tropics as if the broad day had lasted forever." |
| ***Excursions*, 41.31–34**<br><br>Wachusett is, in fact, the observatory of the state. There lay Massachusetts, spread out before us in its length and breadth, like a map. | Charles Theodore Russell. ***The History of Princeton,*** (Boston: Henry P. Lewis, 1838), 27.<br><br>"To the observer from the top, the whole state lies spread out like a map." |
| ***Excursions*, 41.34–42.11**<br><br>There was the level horizon, which told of the sea on the east and south, the well-known hills of New Hampshire on the north and the misty summits of the Hoosac and Green Mountains … blue and unsubstantial …. But Monadnock, rearing its masculine front in the north-west, is the grandest feature. | Charles Theodore Russell. ***The History of Princeton,*** (Boston: Henry P. Lewis, 1838), 27.<br><br>"The neighboring hills, sinking into comparative insignificance, present an even outline to the beholder. On the one hand, is visible the harbor, distant, in the nearest point, forty-eight miles. On the other, the Monadnock is seen rearing its bald and broken summit to the clouds, while the distant Hoosick and Green mountains fade away in the distance, and mingle with the blue horizon." |

| "A Walk to Wachusett" | Source / Statement |
|---|---|
| ***Excursions*, 44.11–21**<br><br>On beholding a picture of a New England village as it then appeared, with a fair open prospect, and a light on trees and river, as if it were broad noon, we find we had not thought the sun shone in those days, or that men lived in broad daylight then. We do not imagine the sun shining on hill and valley during Philip's war, nor on the war-path of Paugus, or Standish, or Church, or Lovell, with serene summer weather, but a dim twilight or night did those events transpire in. They must have fought in the shade of their own dusky deeds. | ***Journal Volume 1*, 417.10–20.** Entry transcribed 1842.<br><br>I find on seeing a painting of our village as it appeared a hundred years ago with a fair open aspect–and a light on trees and river, as if it were mid noon–that I had not thought the sun shone in those days–or that men lived in broad day light then. When I have been reading the Indian wars or the early history of the colonies, I do not remember to have seen the sun once–but a dim twilight or night did their events transpire in. I cannot imagine the sun shining on hill or valley during Philip's war–or on the war path of Paugus–or Standish or Church or Lovell–with serene summer weather. |
| ***Excursions*, 44.22–46.16**<br><br>At length, as we plodded along the dusty roads, our thoughts became as dusty as they; all thought indeed stopped, thinking broke down, or proceeded only passively in a sort of rhythmical cadence of the confused material of thought, and we found ourselves mechanically repeating some familiar measure which timed with our tread; some verse of the Robin Hood ballads, for instance, which one can recommend to travel by.<br><br>"Sweavens are swift, sayd lyttle John,<br>As the wind blows over the hill;<br>For if it be never so loud this night,<br>To-morrow it may be still."<br><br>And so it went up hill and down till a stone interrupted the line, when a new verse was chosen.<br><br>"His shoote it was but loosely shot,<br>Yet flewe not the arrowe in vaine,<br>For it met one of the sheriffe's men,<br>And William-a-Trent was slaine.<br><br>.... Refreshed by this instance of generosity, no less than by the substantial viands set | ***Journal Volume 2*, 377.19–378.17.** No specific date. Entry is in the chapter entitled "Winter 1846-1847." Clearly this is not a source reference, but a reverse. Material for this journal entry that is sourced from the final lines of "A Walk to Wachusett."<br><br>"Robin Hood ballads, for instance, which I can recommend to travel by. Sweavens are swift, sayd little John, ... And so it went up hill & down till a stone interrupted the line, when a new verse was chosen ... There is, however, this consolation to the most way worn traveler, upon the dustiest road, that the path his feet describe is so perfectly symbolical of human life–now climbing hills, now descending into the vales ... Without stopping to tell all of our adventures let it suffice to say that we reached the banks of the Concord on the third morning after our departure–before the sun had climbed many degrees into the heavens<br>And now when we look again Westward from the hills of concord Wachusett and Monadnock have retreated once more among the blue & fabulous mts of the horizon–through our eyes rest on the very rocks where we boiled our hasty pudding amid the clouds." |

| "A Walk to Wachusett" | Source / Statement |
|---|---|
| before him, he pushed forward with new vigor, and reached the banks of the Concord before the sun had climbed many degrees into the heavens." | |
| ***Excursions*, 45.5–14**<br><br>There is, however, this consolation to the most way-worn traveller, upon the dustiest road, that the path his feet describe is so perfectly symbolical of human life-now climbing the hills, now descending into the vales. From the summits he beholds the heavens and the horizon, from the vales he looks up to the heights again. He is treading his old lessons still, and though he may be very weary and travel-worn, it is yet sincere experience. | ***Journal Volume 1*, 435.28–436.1.** Entry dated "Tuesday Aug 9th 1842."<br><br>"There is then much to console the most wayworn traveler upon the dustiest and dullest road that the path his feet travel is so perfectly typical of human life. Now climbing the highest mountains now descending into the lowest vales. From the summits we see the heavens and the horizon from the vales we look up to the heights again." |
| ***Excursions*, 45.21–29**<br>There was such a repose and quiet here at his hour, as if the very hill-sides were enjoying the scene, and as we passed slowly along, looking back over the country we had traversed, and listening to the evening song of the robin, we could not help contrasting the equanimity of nature with the bustle and impatience of man. His words and actions presume always a crisis near at hand, but she is forever silent and unpretending. | ***Journal Volume 1*, 303.22–28.** Entry dated "April 25th 1841."<br><br>"When I hear a robin sing at sunset–I cannot help contrasting the equanimity of nature with the bustle and impatience of man. We return from the lyceum and caucus with such stir and excitement–as if a crisis were at hand but no natural scene or sound sympathizes with us, for nature is always silent and unpretending as at the break of day. She but rubs her eyelids." |
| ***Excursions*, 45.30–46.3**<br>And now that we have returned to the desultory life of the plain, let us endeavor to import a little of that mountain grandeur into it. We will remember within what walls we lie, and understand that this level life too has its summit, and why from the mountain-top the deepest valleys have a tinge of blue; that there is elevation in every hour, as no part of the earth is so low that the heavens may not be seen from it, and we have only to stand on the summit of our hour to command an uninterrupted horizon. | ***Journal Volume 1*, 266.12–17**. Entry dated "Feb. 15th 1841."<br><br>"There is elevation in every hour. No part of the earth is so low and withdrawn, that the heavens cannot be seen from it, but every part supports the sky. We have only to stand on the eminence of the hour, and look out thence into the empyrean, allowing no pinnacle above us, to command an interrupted horizon." |

# Appendix—Published Elevations

### Chronological Sequence by Date of Publication

| Year of Publication | Author/Publication | Source/ Method of determining the height | Height of summit above sea level |
|---|---|---|---|
| ?? | Hon. John Winthrop, Esq; L.L.D.<br>Unknown publication | ?? | 3,012' (several references call out Winthrop as having determined the height to be 3,012' —see below.) |
| 1793 | Rev. Peter Whitney *History of Worcester County* | Winthrop | "its height is 3012 feet above the level of the sea, as was found by the Hon. John Winthrop, Esq; L.L.D. in the year 1777: and this must be 1800 or 1900 feet above the level of the adjacent country." |
| 1821 | Timothy Dwight *Travels; in New England and New York*<br>(A four volume collection) | Winthrop | "This mountain was estimated by the Honorable John Winthrop, LLD. Professor of Mathematics and Natural Philosophy in Harvard College, to be three thousand and twelve feet above the level of the ocean. This estimate is, I suspect, at least five hundred feet higher than the truth." (Vol I, p. 373–374)<br>*and in Volume II, he referred to Hon.* ***James*** *Winthrop ... the same? He indicated that this was the same person.*<br>"[Princeton village stands on a hill] which the Hon. James Winthrop determined to be more than 1,200 feet above the level of the ocean. From this |

| Year of Publication | Author/Publication | Source/ Method of determining the height | Height of summit above sea level |
|---|---|---|---|
| | | | ground, the prospect is very extensive .... Wachusett; a single eminence of an obtuse, conical figure .... The height of this mountain, as determined by the same gentleman, is 3,012 feet above the level of the ocean. It is visible throughout a great part of this State, and in many places in the neighboring States. (Vol. II, p. 261) |
| 1825 (diary 1630-1649) | Hon John Winthrop, Esq., *The History of New England*<br>Ed. by James Savage | Visual | "a very high hill, due west, about forty miles off ...." |
| 1838 | Charles Theodore Russell, *History of Princeton*, Vol I<br>(Vol II is comprised of genealogical records.) | Whitney | "The general elevation of the circumjacent country is 1100 feet. The mountain rears its conical head 1900 feet higher, making its total elevation above Massachusetts Bay, 3000 feet." Also "The prospect from this mountain, of a clear summer morning, is delightful in the extreme." |
| 1839 | John Hayward, *The New England Gazetteer* | Whitney? / Russell? | "Wachusett is 2,990 feet in height ...." |
| 1839 | John Warner Barber, *Historical Collection ... History and antiquities of Every Town in Massachusetts with Geographical descriptions* | Whitney /Russell | "It is a little more than 3,000 feet above the level of the sea, and rises, without any steep ascent, about 1,900 feet higher than the surrounding country." |

| Year of Publication | Author/Publication | Source/ Method of determining the height | Height of summit above sea level |
|---|---|---|---|
| 1843 | Henry D. Thoreau<br>"A Walk to Wachusett" | Russell | "It is but nineteen hundred feet above the village of Princeton, and three thousand above the level of the sea …." |
| ~1840's | Aaron Greenwood *Aaron Greenwood Diaries* –see Page A6-A62. W. M. Sinclair, *Wachusett Gatherings.* | Calculation by triangulation | 959 ft above "Uncle Nat's Pond" including 31 feet correction for the earth's curvature gives a height of 2,024' |
| 1847 | John Hayward, *Gazetteer of Massachusetts* | Russell/ Barometric | "This mountain rears its conical head two thousand and eighteen feet above Massachusetts Bay." "rears its conical head" comes from Russell; unknown source of the 2018 elevation. |
| 1852 | Rev. Jeremiah Lyford Hanaford<br>*History of Princeton* | Winthrop/ Russell | "its height is 3012 feet above the level of Massachusetts Bay, as found by actual survey, in 1777, by Hon. John Winthrop." Also mentioned: circumjacent country is 1100' and "conical head" is 1900' above the country. |
| 1854 | John Hayward<br>*Gazetteer of the United States of America* | Russell/ Barometric | "This mountain rears its conical head two thousand and eighteen feet above Massachusetts Bay, and the prospect from the top is delightful." |
| 1857 | William Baker<br>Map of Princeton | Unknown | The summit indication on Bakers map shows 2018 ft. |

| **Year of Publication** | **Author/Publication** | **Source/ Method of determining the height** | **Height of summit above sea level** |
|---|---|---|---|
| 1884 | S. C. Bullard<br>(From U.S. survey documents.) *Guide to Wachusett Mountain, Princeton, Mass.* see Page A65–A66, Warren M. Sinclair, *Wachusett Gatherings.* | Unknown | 2,480' from Coast Survey Results in 1860. |
| 1915 | Francis Everette Blake,<br>*History of Princeton, Massachusetts* | Hayward? / Baker Map? | "Wachusett mountain, the principal elevation and most striking feature in this town, raised to a height of 2018 feet." |
| 2006 | Commonwealth of Massachusetts, Dept of Environmental Management. | | 2,006' |

# Appendix—Highway Directions

Cumulative miles are provided between brackets. This is the route taken by Thoreau and Fuller. The full route may be traveled on foot; it can be driven with the exceptions noted in items 4 and 33.

1. **[0.00 mi.]** Begin at the Emerson House, 28 Cambridge Turnpike, Concord, Massachusetts. Go northwest on Cambridge Turnpike toward Lexington Rd/Rt. 2A. Head to Concord Center. Slight left at Lexington Rd/Rt. 2A. Continue to Monument Square **[.41 mi.]**

2. Turn left at Main St/Rt. 2A/Rt. 62. Stay on Main St; pass the Public Library. Cross Sudbury River **[1.45 mi.]** (South Bridge). Go beneath RR tracks.

3. Stay left at the fork of Rt. 62 and Rt. 2A. Stay on Main St/Rt. 62 (Rt. 2A /Elm St go to the right). Cross Rt. 2. Cross the Assabet as you enter West Concord **[2.58 mi.]** Continue on Rt. 62 at the fork where Commonwealth Ave goes to the Right.

4. Take a right at Old Stow Road **[3.50 mi.]**—a winding road, it goes up the hill and crosses over the RR tracks on the Old Stow Road Bridge. At the top of the hill, take a left and follow the dirt path into the woods. Do not continue on Hillside Ave. You are on the Old Road to Stow—now abandoned and overgrown.

*[If driving, continue on Hillside ¼ mi until you reach Laws Brook Road–turn left and go about ¾ mi farther. Parker Street is on the left. Turn left until you cross the RR tracks (.8 mi.). Continue until you reach Independence Road on your left—another ½ mile. You are now back on the route for "A Walk to Wachusett.]*

5. Follow the tracks and cross them to make your way to Independence Rd.

6. Continue on Independence until you reach Parker St. **[5.20 mi.]**

7. Follow Parker St south, cross Rt. 27; continue southward (1 ½ mi) until you reach Summer St. **[6.84 mi.]**

8. Take a right at Summer St. Follow Summer St. After ½ mi. you will go up a hill (Pompositticut Hill). Continue down the other side until you reach Rt. 117—The Great Road—Rt. 62. **[8.3 mi.]**

9. Stay on 117 (NOTE: Rt. 62 goes left at Upper Stow Common—do NOT take it.) Stay on Rt. 117.

10. Cross Great Brook; pass Bolton Farm Orchards; pass Bolton Pan Cemetery (on the right); go beneath Rt. 495 Overpass **[14.53 mi.]** Go through Bolton Center until you get to the blinking light **[15.5 mi.]**—Wattaquadock Hill Road.

11. Take a left at Wattaquadock Hill Road. Bear to the right as you go up the hill and past Nashoba Valley Winery (on your left).

12. Take a right at Old Bay Road- up and over the top of Wataquadock where Thoreau and Fuller rested at mid-day.

13. At the intersection of Old Bay Road and Wilder **[17.21 mi.]**, follow Wilder Road past the golf course. Careful, this is a tricky intersection. Pass Eastwood Cemetery (on your right) as you get farther down the hill where the name changes to Old Common road. Continue to intersection with Rt. 110.

14. Reputed to be one of the most dangerous intersections in Lancaster, this is the intersection of five roads, and only a blinking red light to serve as a precautionary warning. Stop at the gas station/convenience store **[18.81 mi.]** for refreshment.

15. Take Bolton Road—from the intersection—the South Branch of the Nashua. This is the Intervale—stay straight until you reach Main St., South Lancaster. **[19.93 mi.]** Atlantic Union College will be across Main Street to your right.

16. Go left on Main—Cross Main Street—*go about 100 yards*—locate Sterling Road. **[20.79 mi.]**

17. Follow Sterling Road—stay to the right—after a short distance you will see Deershorn Road run off to the left. D*o not take Deershorn Road.* This is the area of Lancaster known as Ebenville. Go down hill and cross the RR tracks, coming up on the other side to Rt. 62 or the Clinton road. On the left, after about 100 yards, stop and have an ice cream at the Sterling Ice Cream stand. **[21.84 mi.]**

18. Stay on Rt. 62 past Hillside Cemetery and Oak Hill Cemetery—all the way to Sterling Center. **[24.40 mi.]**

19. Main St. Sterling—have a snack at one of the pizza shops or markets in town.

20. Follow signs for Rt. 62. Bear to the right and go up the hill about 150 yards past the town green. Go under Interstate Rt 190.

21. At the top of the hill, take a right on to Beamon Road (Careful—not Osgood Road).

22. Do not follow Rt. 62 which is Princeton Road—it goes to the left..

23. Take Beamon Road until you hit the N. Oakdale Cutoff—bear left. You are at the intersection with Redemption Rock Road. **[27.82 mi.]** This is the site of the old Buss Inn and Tavern where Thoreau spent the first night.

Explore the wooded lot on the right hand side of the intersection (don't cross Redemption Rock Road–Rt. 140). You will quickly find the old cellar holes of the Inn and the barn.

24. Take a right turn after the intersection; follow Redemption Rock Road north. The Stillwater River runs on your left as you head north.

25. After 1.75 miles, just before you enter East Princeton, you will notice a sharp drop-off to a deep ravine—on your left. That is the ravine of which Thoreau wrote in the essay. **[29.57 mi.]**

26. As you leave East Princeton, at the intersection of Redemption Rock Road with Route 31, continue across the intersection, following Beamon Road. This road is a paved two-lane road that winds through the forested countryside.

27. Follow the road for 2 miles—do not turn right at Wilder Road—eventually you will start to descend a long hill. At the bottom, you will intersect (a T intersection—Beamon ends here.) Mirick Road. **[32.28 mi.]** The intersection represents the "Base of the Mountain." A swampy area sits across the other side of the road.

28. Take a right on Mirick; go for 1/3 of a mile winding up to a farmhouse on your right with its red barn on your left; the road will then go down a slight grade and cross a stream. A small orchard will be on the other side of a high stone fence on your left. At the end of the orchard will be Gregory Road. **[32.58 mi.]**

29. Take a left at Gregory Road—steep and narrow—barely enough for one vehicle.

30. Follow Gregory as it winds up through a grove of Maple trees. At the end of the steep incline, it will intersect Mountain Road. A parking lot will be on the left as you reach the intersection. **[33.11 mi.]** Now you have to walk!

31. Cross the road and take a left for about 25 yards at which point you will see the entrance to the Wachusett Mountain State Reservation via the Mountain House Trail.

32. Follow the trail up for about 1 mile—do not take any other trails even as they join with the Mountain House Trail.

33. Next stop— the Summit!!!! **[33.92 mi.]**

*[It is possible to drive to the summit. From item 31, turn right on Mountain Road and drive north for about a mile. You will see the entrance and the road to the summit. There is now an entry fee. Enjoy the sights both near and far as you wind your way to the top. Picnic benches with information signs frequent the drive. I have noted over the years that they are very well used. Enjoy your visit.]*

# Selected Bibliography

## Text Materials Cited or Referenced

Alden, Peter et al. (Cassie, Brian; Forster, Richard; Keen, Richard; Leventer, Amy; Zomlefer, Wendy B.). *National Audubon Society Field Guide to New England.* New York: Alfred A. Knoph, 1998.

Anderson, Joyce Bailey. *Images of America, Princeton and Wachusett Mountain.* Charleston, S.C.: Arcadia, 2003.

Anderson, Robert C. *Directions of a Town: The History of Harvard, Massachusetts.* Harvard: Harvard Common, 1976.

Barrett, Ella V., et al. *History of Bolton: 1738–1938.* Bolton: Town of Bolton, 1938.

Barber, John Warner. *Historical Collections, being a general collection of Interesting Facts, traditions, biographical sketches, anecdotes, &c., Relating to the History and antiquities of Every Town in Massachusetts with Geographical descriptions.* Worcester: Dorr, Howand, 1839.

Blake, Francis Everett Blake. *History of Princeton Massachusetts.* vol.I. Boston: Blake, 1915.

Bulfinch, Thomas. *The Age of Fable – Stories of Gods and Heroes.* Greenwich, Connecticut: Fawcett, 1961.

Childs, Ethel B. *History of Stow, Tercentenary, 1883–1983.* Stow, Massachusetts: Stow Historical Society, 1983.

Collingwood, R. G. *The Idea of History.* ed. Jan Van Der Dussen. rev. ed. New York: Oxford UP, 1994.

Forbes, Ann McCarthy. *Narrative Histories of Concord and West Concord.* Concord: Concord Historical Commission, 1995.

———. *West Concord: Survey of Historical and Architectural Resources.* Concord: Concord Historical Commission, 1989.

Fuller, Richard. "Visit to the Wachusett," *The Thoreau Society Bulletin 121.* (Fall 1972), 1–4.

Garber, Frederick. *Thoreau's Redemptive Imagination.* New York: NYU Press, 1977.

Harding, Walter and Michael Meyer. *The New Thoreau Handbook*, New York: New York University Press, 1980.

Hanaford, Jeremiah Lyford. *History of Princeton, Worcester County, Massachusetts, Civil and Ecclesiastical: from its First Settlement in 1739 to April 1852.* Worcester: C. Backingham Webb, 1852.

Harding, Walter. *The Days of Henry Thoreau: A Biography.* New York: Dover, 1982.

Hayward, John. *The New England Gazetteer.* 2nd ed. Boston: Hayward, 1839.

Hill, Leonard. *Hill's Meteorological and Chronological Register.* Plymouth, Massachusetts, 1869.

Howarth, William. ed. and commentary, *Thoreau in the Mountains.* New York: Farrar, 1982.

———. ed. and commentary, *Walking With Thoreau, A Literary Guide to the Mountains of New England.* Boston: Beacon, 2001.

Joslin, Elmer L. *Notes on the acceptance or Layouts of Public Ways.* Concord Public Library, Special Collections, 1956.

Lennon, Heather Maurer. *Images of America, Lancaster.* Charleston, SC: Arcadia, 2001.

Loewer, Peter. *Thoreau's Garden: Native Plants for the American Landscape.* Mechanicsburg, Pennsylvania: Stackpole, 1996.

Marlowe, George Francis. *The Old Bay Paths: Their Villages and Byways and their Stories.* New York: Hastings House. 1942.

Marvin, Abijah P. *History of the Town of Lancaster, Massachusetts: From the First Settlement to the Present Time 1643 –1879.* Lancaster: Town of Lancaster. 1879.

Maynard, W. Barksdale. *Walden Pond, A History.* New York: Oxford UP, 2004.

Meltzer, Milton and Walter Harding. *A Thoreau Profile*, Concord: Thoreau Foundation. 1962.

Miller, Perry. *Consciousness in Concord.* Boston: Houghton Mifflin, 1958.

Nourse, Henry S. *History of the Town of Harvard, Massachusetts, 1732–1893.* Harvard: Warren Hapgood, 1894.

Phalen, Harold R. *History of the Town of Acton.* Cambridge, Massachusetts: Middlesex Printing, 1954.

Richardson, Robert D. *Henry Thoreau: The Life of a Mind.* Los Angeles: University California P, 1986.

Russell, Charles Theodore. *The History of Princeton, Worcester County, Massachusetts.* Boston: Lewis, 1838.

Sanborn, F. B. *The Life of Henry David Thoreau.* Boston: Houghton, 1917.

Stafford, Mary Fuller. *Story of Colonial Lancaster.* Rutland, Vt.: Tuttle, 1937.

Sattelmeyer, Robert. *Thoreau's Reading: A Study in Intellectual History with Bibliographical Catalogue.* Princeton: Princeton UP, 1988.

Sinclair, Warren M. *Wachusett: Wajuset Gatherings From Then and When.* Salem, Ma.: Higginson Book, 1996.

Thoreau, Henry David. *A Week on the Concord and Merrimack Rivers.* Princeton: Princeton UP, 1980.

———. *The Best of Thoreau's Journals.* ed. Carl Bode. Carbondale: Southern Illinois UP, 1967.

———. *Consciousness in Concord, The Text of Thoreau's Hitherto "Lost Journal" (1840–1841) Together with Notes and a Commentary.* ed. Perry Miller. Boston: Houghton, 1958.

———. *Excursions.* ed. Joseph Moldenhauer. Princeton: Princeton UP, 2007.

———. *The Heart of Thoreau's Journals.* ed. Odell Shepard, New York: Dover, 1961, revised version of Mifflin, 1927.

———. *Henry David Thoreau: Collected Essays and Poems.* ed. Elizabeth Hall Witherell. New York: Literary Classics, 2001.

———. *Elevating Ourselves: Thoreau on Mountains.* ed. J. Parker Huber. Boston: Houghton, 1999.

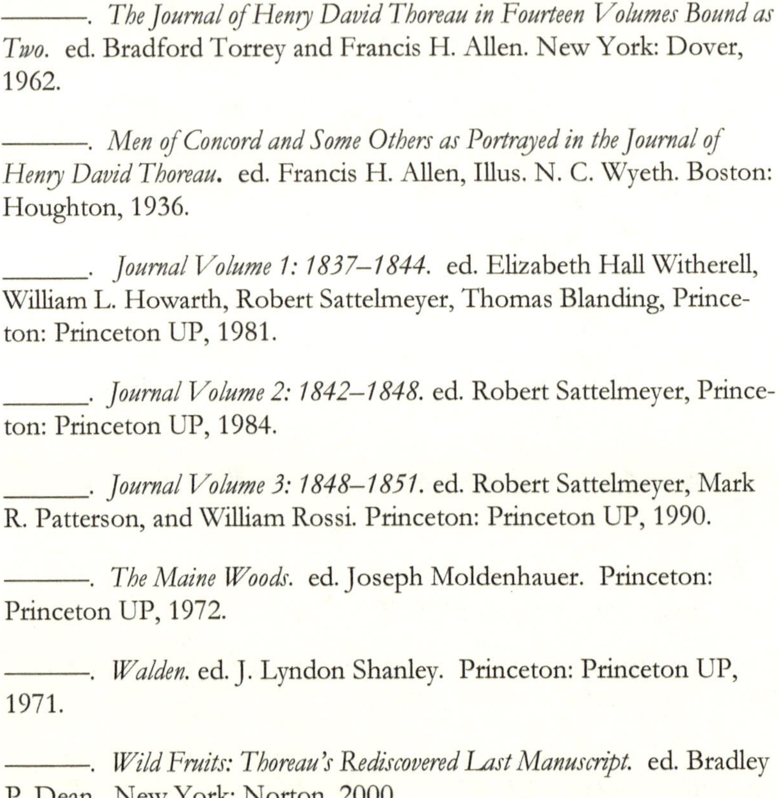

———. *The Journal of Henry David Thoreau in Fourteen Volumes Bound as Two.* ed. Bradford Torrey and Francis H. Allen. New York: Dover, 1962.

———. *Men of Concord and Some Others as Portrayed in the Journal of Henry David Thoreau.* ed. Francis H. Allen, Illus. N. C. Wyeth. Boston: Houghton, 1936.

______. *Journal Volume 1: 1837–1844.* ed. Elizabeth Hall Witherell, William L. Howarth, Robert Sattelmeyer, Thomas Blanding, Princeton: Princeton UP, 1981.

______. *Journal Volume 2: 1842–1848.* ed. Robert Sattelmeyer, Princeton: Princeton UP, 1984.

______. *Journal Volume 3: 1848–1851.* ed. Robert Sattelmeyer, Mark R. Patterson, and William Rossi. Princeton: Princeton UP, 1990.

———. *The Maine Woods.* ed. Joseph Moldenhauer. Princeton: Princeton UP, 1972.

———. *Walden.* ed. J. Lyndon Shanley. Princeton: Princeton UP, 1971.

———. *Wild Fruits: Thoreau's Rediscovered Last Manuscript.* ed. Bradley P. Dean. New York: Norton, 2000.

Tougias, Michael J. *New England Wild Places*, North Attleborough: Covered Bridge, 1997.

Walcott, Charles H. *Concord in the Colonial Period, being a history of the town of Concord, Massachusetts.* Boston: Estes, 1884.

Warren, Francis W. *Recollections of Stow*, Stow: Stow Historical Society, 1990.

Whitney, Peter. *The History of The County of Worcester, in the Commonwealth of Massachusetts.* Thomas: Worcester, 1793.

Winthrop, John, Esq., *The History of New England from 1630 to 1649.* ed. James Savage. Boston: Massachusetts Historical Society, Phelps, 1825.

## Email

Baker, Doug. Email to the author dated 8/29/2005 concerning the First Parish Bell.

Howarth, William. Email to the author dated 6/29/2004 relative to his trip from Concord to Wachusett.

Marques, Peter R. Email to the author dated 10/11/2005 concerning various tent styles and fabrics used in the Thoreau era. Principle of website Tentsmiths.com

Moldenhauer, Joseph. Email to the author dated 8/4/2008 relative to sources used by Thoreau in *Excursions*.

Otterberg, Henrik. Email to the author dated 8/16/2006 relative to the Swedish Inn quote.

Sattelmeyer, Robert. Email to the author dated 8/13/2006 on possible sources of text and on the Swedish Inn quotation.

## Software

Asynx Planetarium v1.33, computer software, Thousand Oaks, Ca.: Asynx Software, 2005.

National Geographic—Northeastern, USA, maps powered by TOPO!, computer software, San Francisco: National Geographic, 2002.

## Websites

Bartlett, John Russell. *Dictionary of Americanisms*. NY: Bartlett and Welford, 1848.
<http://www.merrycoz.org/voices/bartlett/AMER11.htm>

Boberg, Carl. Hymn, *How Great Thou Art*, Swedish folk melody, "O Store Gud." Verse 2 and refrain. [cited 6/3/08]<http://en.wikipedia.org/wiki/ How_Great_Thou_Art>.

Daylight Savings Time Web Exhibit.
<http://webexhibits.org/daylightsaving/index.html>

Ells, Stephen. *Stephen ells' Thoreau etc. research page*. Thoreau Country: Location Note. [cited: 7/10/08] <http://homepage.mac.com/sfe/henry/country_ not_esta/concord-river.htm>

Gottfred, A. "Tents of the Northwest Fur Trade," Northwest Journal, Fur Trade Tents, [cited February 2007].
<http://www.northwestjournal.ca>

Griffin, David. "A History of the Maynard Post Office," Maynard Historical Society, n.d. [cited May 3, 2006]. <http://web.maynard.ma.us/history/founders /founders.htm>.

Hazlitt, William. "Why Distant Objects Please" in *Table-Talk: Essays on Men and Manners* (1822). <http://www.blupete.com/Literature/ Essays/Hazlitt/TableTalk/.htm>.

Hayward, John. *Gazetteer of the Unites States of America.* Philadelphia: Gihon, 1854. <http://books.google.com/books>

———. *The Massachusetts Gazetteer.* Boston: Hayward, 1847. <http://books.google.com/books>

*The Legend of Lucy Keyes.* [cited March 2007] <http://www.lucykeyes.com/lucy/legend/lucy_disappears.shtml>

Margaret Fuller Chronology. [Cited 2006]. <http://courses.washington.edu/hum523/fuller/Chronology.shtml>

McGonigle, Kyle. *Early 1800 Army tents and the Decision of 1843.* <http://www. dodgenet.com/~ghostgar/1800ArmyTents.html>

Prince Seraphim or The Fallen Angel. Cambridge University Magazine. Volume II, London: W.P. Grant, 1843. p 69. [cited January 2008]. <http://books.google.com/books>

Providence and Worcester Railroad Company. About Us. <http://www. pwrr.com/PWmap2.html>

Shattuck, Lemuel. *History of the town of Concord: Middlesex County, Massachusetts from its earliest settlement to1832.* <http://users.rcn.com/greenela/id62.htm#history_of_acton>

Tentsmiths on Tents. Tentsmiths provides information on period history tents, specifically conical tents as Thoreau used. <http://www.tentsmiths.com>

Thomson, Thomas. *Travels in Sweden During the Autumn of 1812.* London: Baldwin, 1813. Digitized by Google. July 2007. <http://books.google.com/books>

Thoreau, Henry David. *Land and Property Surveys: Acton/Concord Town Line … [Sept. 15, 1851].* The Concord Free Public Library, Special Collections: Concord, 2005. [cited Oct2004] <http://www.concordlibrary.org/scollect/Thoreau_surveys/1.htm>

Town of Bolton. *Town of Bolton, 1998 Historical Properties Survey.* Transportation Routes (1776-1830). <http://www.townofbolton.com/Pages/BotonMA_Town History/toc>

Town of Bolton. *Bolton Reconnaissance Report*, Massachusetts Heritage Landscape Inventory Program, June 2006. <http://www.townofbolton.com>

US Naval Observatory. *Data Services* <http://aa.usno.navy.mil/data/>

**Miscellaneous Documents and Sources**

*A Brief History of Sterling, Massachusetts.* Held by Sterling Public Library. Sterling: Town of Sterling, 1931.

Inventory Form continuation Sheet, Historical Narrative for *Sterling, Pottery Village,* Massachusetts Historical Commission, Massachusetts Archives, copy held by Sterling Historical Society.

Kruger, James. "Walk to Wachusetts [sic]." The Thoreau Institute at Walden Woods, Walter Harding Collection, Series II.5.c.3.a–d.

Walcott, Charles H. *Concord Roads, notes by*, 1938. The Concord Free Public Library, Special Collections. Charles H. Walcott Papers, Series II: Foldered Materials, Folder II, 2.10.

Young, Robert. *Wachusett Chronologically–I.* Unpublished journal. 2001

Young, Robert. Transcript tape of August 2005 trip; "Walking to Wachusett." 2008.

Maps and Sketches in a pamphlet compiled by the Acton Historical Commission, no date. Held by Acton Public Library.

**Maps**

Atlas of Worcester County, New York: Beers, 1870, reprint Rutland, Vt.: Tuttle, 1971. Historical Map of Acton, Tuttle MDCCCXC (1980). Copy held by Acton Public Library, Acton, Massachusetts. Ma.

Brown, Jabez, surveyor. A plan of the town of Acton in November 1794, Ref 974.44, A188, #2. Copy held by Acton Public Library, Acton, Massachusetts. Ma.

A Town Map of Lancaster drawn up in 1795 –from Abijah P. Marvin, *History of the Town of Lancaster, Massachusetts: From the First Settlement to the Present Time: 1643-1879.* Lancaster: Town of Lancaster, 1879.

Merriam, Amos. Princeton survey and map, 1830. Copy held by Princeton Historical Society, Princeton, Massachusetts.

Sawyer, Moses. 1830 Survey of Sterling, Pendleton's Lithography, Boston, from the *Atlas of Worcester County*.

# Index

# About the Author

Robert Young, a native son of Massachusetts, grew up in White River Junction, Vermont, attending schools of the Town of Hartford. From the hills of Vermont, he headed south to the University of North Carolina in Chapel Hill where he was graduated in 1967 with a degree in Mathematics and a commission as an Ensign in the U.S. Navy. With the military, he traveled extensively in the Far East until he resigned his commission in 1972. Married to Kathleen in 1970, the Young's have two daughters.

In 1972, he began a successful career in manufacturing, settling in South Bound Brook, New Jersey. Since then they have resided in West Hartford, Connecticut and most recently in Leominster, Massachusetts. There, he earned a Master of Business Administration degree from Nichols College located in Dudley, Massachusetts.

Young enjoys his family, including two grandsons, hiking, amateur radio, and reading. He can be reached at ryoung@alumni.unc.edu.

# Reader's Notes:

www.ingramcontent.com/pod-product-compliance
Lightning Source LLC
LaVergne TN
LVHW090936080826
845145LV00003B/773

*9780615264080*